COOL careers for girls

as

Crime Solvers

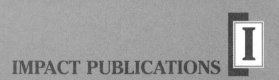

IMPACT PUBLICATIONS

COOL
careers
for
girls

as

Crime
Solvers

LINDA THORNBURG

Library of Congress Cataloging-in-Publication Data

Thornburg, Linda, 1949-
    Cool careers for girls as crime solvers / Linda Thornburg.
        p. cm.
Includes bibliographical references and index.
Summary: Profiles ten women with careers in different areas of crime solving, including firearms examiner, forensic anthropologist, and latent fingerprint examiner, and explains their duties and how they prepared for and got their positions.
    ISBN 1-57023-175-3 (hardcover) -- ISBN 1-57023-174-5 (paperback)
    1. Criminal investigation--Vocational guidance--United States--Juvenile literature. 2. Forensic sciences--Vocational guidance--United States--Juvenile literature. 3. Women forensic scientists--United States--Juvenile literature. {1. Criminal investigation--Vocational guidance. 2. Forensic sciences--Vocational guidance. 3. Women forensic scientists. 4. Vocational guidance.} I. Title.
HV8073.8.T56 2001
363.25'023'73--dc21

                    2001039988

Publisher: For information on Impact Publications, including current and forthcoming publications, authors, press kits, bookstore, and submission requirements, visit Impact's Web site: www.impactpublications.com

Publicity/Rights: For information on publicity, author interviews, and subsidiary rights, contact the Public Relations and Marketing Department: Tel. 703/361-7300 or Fax 703/335-9486.

Sales/Distribution: All paperback bookstore sales are handled through Impact's trade distributor: National Book Network, 15200 NBN Way, Blue Ridge Summit, PA 17214, Tel. 1-800-462-6420. All other sales and distribution inquiries should be directed to the publisher: Sales Department, IMPACT PUBLICATIONS, 9104-N Manassas Dr., Manassas Park, VA 20111-5211, Tel. 703/361-7300, Fax 703/335-9486, or E-mail: coolcareers@impactpublications.com

Book design by Guenet Abraham
Desktopped by C. M. Grafik

Dedicated to the women who were

kind enough to share their stories

in this book

Contents

A Special Introduction by Dr. Marcella F. Fierro

Chief Medical Examiner of the Commonwealth of Virginia

Like science? Then here are jobs for you! Forensic science and forensic medicine are wonderful worlds for women. The forensic disciplines are the sciences of the "forum" or court. They share interesting work, lots of action, and lifelong learning. In this book you will read about women working in forensic science and medicine, as well as in other jobs where crime solving is key. A forensic scientist's love of science, enthusiasm, and strong sense of integrity make going to the lab each workday a new adventure. Right now there is a need for 9,000 forensic scientists across the country, and medical examiners' and coroners' offices are actively seeking forensic pathologists.

What do these women of science do? They answer questions! Lots of questions! Questions about how someone died and if the death was due to natural disease, poisoning, or violent causes. If the decedent was a victim of violence, can DNA match the assailant? Is there a match by fingerprints? By trace evidence left at a crime scene? Can a forged will be detected? Can bones tell the life and identity of a person? Can a police forensic artist capture a criminal's or unknown skull's visage? How can a computer criminal be traced? Does the bullet recovered from a victim match the weapon belonging to a suspect? Does material recovered from a burned out warehouse show gasoline as evidence of arson? Is the white powder recovered by a crime scene investigator cocaine, heroin, or a headache powder? Is the claim for accident insurance payment being sought for an honest accident or is it a fraud? All these women work to answer the questions about what happened. They are medical and scientific detectives. The homicide detective, fraud investigator, and prosecutors work with these forensic detectives to answer the question of who did it and why.

Can you become a forensic pathologist, forensic scientist, forensic investigator, or forensic artist? Certainly, why not? What does it take? How do you find out and how do you prepare? This book will answer some of these questions.

My own introduction to the world of forensic medicine began in elementary school with an interest in the natural sciences—reading science books and going to the science museum. This evolved in high school to a fascination with the biological sciences. By college I knew my interest in biology and my desire to care for people meant I must be a physician. Life choices were easy after that: it either fit with the long-term plan to be a doctor or it was out. Medical school was a little lonesome in those days. My class graduated 4 women and 84 men. Now half the medical students across the country are women and the atmosphere is collegial.

The next step was to decide on a special field of interest—medical or surgical specialties or family practice. Although I enjoyed all my rotations in surgery, internal medicine, pediatrics, and obstetrics, I was drawn to the puzzle-solving aspects of pathology.

Pathologists are physicians who serve as consultants to their fellow physicians by answering questions in the laboratory. Is this tissue biopsy cancer? Does this blood smear show anemia or leukemia? Does this blood chemistry show diabetes? It is great fun and very, very interesting. Even more interesting is trying to figure out how and why people died, by performing autopsies. Figuring out if a liver abnormality fits with abnormalities of the heart and kidney and if it does, how and why and what disease they represent remains a challenge.

A subspecialty of pathology is forensic pathology. It deals with medical mysteries of cause and manner of death and with the recognition of scientific evidence on the body, whether is a unique patterned injury due to a specific class of weapon, or trace evidence left in or on the body by an assailant. A more complete description of what a forensic pathologist does is included in this book.

Forensic Professionals Are Teachers

As teachers, forensic scientists teach anyone who needs to know about forensic science and medicine. Testifying in court is an exercise in teaching. Forensic scientists explain to judges and juries how and what forensic tests were performed and what they mean, while the forensic pathologist speaks to what abnormalities and injuries were found on the body, what evidence was collected from the body, and how the injury occurred. Forensic crime scene investigators guide the jury through the scene of a criminal event and explain what evidence they recovered. Forensic witnesses give objective scientific evidence that speaks to the what and how of a crime. Their testimony is unbiased and based on science. It is independent of whether the forensic expert was summoned by the prosecution or defense in a criminal case or the plaintiff or defense in a civil case. Insurance fraud investigators and police and homicide detectives gather all the information and work with prosecutors to put it all together to fashion a criminal case. Then, given the impartial information the forensic teacher imparts, the judge and jury can decide if a crime was committed, what type of crime, and what punishment fits the crime. Court work is an important part of the job, and the forensic scientist can expect to spend time conferencing cases with attorneys and testifying in court. Testifying in court also requires language skills sufficient to make the complex understandable and the ability to know the limitations of the specific discipline. If the forensic scientist keeps a sense of the truth close to her heart, then vigorous cross-examination can only enhance the quality of the expert's testimony.

Besides strengths in science and teaching, forensic scientists and forensic pathologists must have a powerful sense of integrity, an absolute commitment to the truth, and the ability to work as part of a forensic team.

Interested? This book is a great place to start learning about careers in forensic science and crime detection. The forensic experts in this book will tell you about their life and work and how to get started. As soon as you can, take science courses so you have a starting point for any of these exciting careers. Speak with your guidance counselor about preparations for careers in forensic science and medicine. Make the acquaintance of forensic pathologists and the forensic scientists in your local or state forensic laboratories. The Discovery and Learning Channels have programs highlighting the work of forensic scientists and forensic pathologists. The National Association of Medical Examiners, on the Internet at www.theNAME.org, has information on forensic pathology and medical examiners. The American Academy of Forensic Sciences at www.aafs.org features a career brochure, a list of undergraduate and master's programs, and information on emerging forensic disciplines.

Here is some information about the various forensic specialties:

Forensic Pathology

The patients of the forensic pathologist are dead, so the forensic pathologist is skilled at making the dead patient tell his story. The forensic pathologist examines patients and performs medicolegal autopsies to determine why people died and if it was violent, what kind of violence. Forensic pathologists, utilizing the body of knowledge of medicine, address issues of cause of death, time of death, lethal versus non-lethal injuries, patterned injuries and the weapons that caused them, interval since injury, and whether the sequence of injury can be reconstructed.

The forensic pathologist performs autopsies as directed by law and that are considered to be in the public interest. Correlating injuries with the information about the circumstances as developed by medical and police investigation allows sorting out a death as natural, or due to accident, suicide, or homicide. For example, a person may be physiologically dead due to a gunshot wound to the head, but the investigation may show circumstances indicating the person was shot by someone else (homicide) or shot himself (suicide), or that the death was due to a weapon malfunction (accident). The forensic pathologist helps identify unidentified dead persons by working with the forensic dentist, the forensic radiologist, the fingerprints examiner, DNA examiner, and forensic anthropologist. Establishing identity is a major part of mass disaster work and is absolutely critical for the families of persons who are burned, decomposed, or skeletonized. The forensic pathologist is the last physician to care for the patient and console the family.

The work is interesting, often unpredictable as to findings, and never routine. An emerging area of forensic pathology is clinical forensic pathology, where the forensic pathologist has the opportunity to examine living survivors of violence to interpret the same patterns of injury as seen in the dead. Record reviews of living patients can assist in sorting out complex violent situations where some victims survive while others die; for example, sorting out the injuries of drivers versus passengers and identifying injuries due to blows versus those sustained in a fall. The forensic pathologist also serves as a public health officer by recognizing diseases that are a hazard to the public health, providing surveillance for unsafe products and preventable injuries, and developing data used for injury prevention.

Forensic Anthropology

The forensic anthropologist is a physical anthropologist with special expertise in skeletal biology and bones. Anthropologists study bones recovered all over the world to tell about the life, work, and health of human beings through the ages. Forensic anthropologists have special experience in dealing with the forensic issues of identity, injury, and diseases of bone. Forensic anthropologists help identify persons by recognizing the characteristics of skeletons or parts of skeletons to tell if the remains are human or animal and if they are of forensic (recent) or historical interest. The forensic anthropologist can tell the sex, race, age, stature, health status, and presence of skeletal disease. They find bullet holes, knife and slash marks, and depressed skull fractures due to blows, and can reconstruct crushed or damaged bones. The forensic anthropologist can differentiate injury that occurred at or about the time of death from old injury or postmortem damage.

Sometimes, working with the forensic team and with the forensic entomologist's information about insect infestation of the remains, the anthropologist can help with determining the time of injury and death. The forensic anthropologist works closely with the forensic pathologist and others in the identification of the dead in mass disasters such as air crashes, floods, and multiple fatality fires. In recent years, forensic anthropologists have assisted in the investigation of human rights violations by identifying victims and their injuries in mass burials due to genocide. Some forensic anthropologists utilize art and science to reconstruct the appearance of an unidentified person by making a clay reconstruction of facial features on an unidentified skull. Others are skilled at computer reconstruction of visage and with aging the appearance of persons missing for years so they can be recognized, as in the case of children missing for years.

Forensic Bloodstain Pattern Analyst

The forensic bloodstain pattern analyst studies the patterns bloodstains make.

Utilizing physics and mathematics the bloodstain analyst can tell the direction, distance, velocity, and point of origin of stains. This forensic scientist can differentiate stains that are drops, drops dropping on other drops, stains transferred from one item to another, and spatters due to impacts. By studying blood stains at scenes the "spatter expert" can sometimes tell where the first blow or stab was struck and follow the progression of a struggle from room to room. The bloodstain pattern analyst is especially helpful at reconstructing bloody scenes. If the pathologist finds a person with a cut artery and the spatter expert finds the pulsatile pattern of arterial bleeding on a wall, they can establish the position of the decedent when he or she received the strike. Reconstruction by interpretation of blood spatter patterns at crime scene may establish the credibility of a suspect's story of self-defense or destroy it with certainty.

Firearms and Tool Mark Examiner

These scientists are the jacks-of-all-trades. If it is a thing and you want to match it, talk with this forensic scientist. They match pry bars with marks of forced entry, cartridge cases to other cartridge cases, and suspect guns. They delve into their magic computers and match casings from crime scenes distant and far. They study bullets recovered from victims of shootings, telling investigators what brands of guns may have fired them and

then match them to suspect guns. They examine clothes to tell the distance from which a weapon was fired and how that varies with the ammunition and powder load. They look at clothes and sort out entrances versus exits. The forensic pathologist works with the firearms examiner to establish that supposedly self-inflicted wounds are indeed within arms reach, and to identify unusual ammunition. Special examinations these scientists perform include raising serial numbers that have been obliterated on guns, fracture matching broken pieces of things to establish they originated from one and the same item, headlamps to see if they were on at the time of an impact, and speedometers to determine speed at impact. If the investigator does not know what to do with something, this examiner will probably figure something out. If the pathologist finds a broken fingernail on a victim and the investigator finds a piece of broken fingernail in a car trunk, this examiner can match the nail ridges, thus proving the nail was likely broken inside the car trunk.

Fingerprint Examiner/Analyst

The fingerprint examiner is an identity expert. By studying the friction ridge patterns of fingertips, toes, and lips left on items, this scientist can say they came from a particular individual. Give this examiner fragments of waterlogged or burned skin from an unidentified fatality and if there is ridge detail to recover, it will be done. This examiner utilizes an automated fingerprint identification system (AFIS) to find a match and establish the identity. Matching fingerprints from crime scenes and from items involved in crimes to known prints of suspects solves many crimes and places a suspect at a scene. Using powders, chemicals, fuming with superglue, and photography, the fingerprint examiner recovers prints and establishes identity. Some examiners also work with impressions such as those of footwear or tires and perform image enhancement to improve the quality of surveillance camera film, blurred images, and other patterns suitable for matching.

Forensic Laboratory Director/Biologist

The lab director is a combination of executive, administrator, policy maker, facilitator and scientist. The director makes forensic science laboratories work. Usually experienced forensic scientists ascend to this position by possessing administrative as well as scientific skills. The director recognizes new technologies and sees that they are implemented by seeing that examiners are trained in the new technologies, that the best equipment is obtained, and that quality assurance programs are in place. The laboratory director is familiar with all the forensic disciplines and facilitates interactions between the disciplines. Budgets and space for forensic laboratories is always tight, and it is the director who establishes the priorities, finds grants,

writes them, and seeks to fund critical needs. The director manages paper and weird subpoenas and prepares reports of workload, performance, and needed resources. The director is a scientist's best friend and advocate.

The forensic biologist is a matchmaker; matching the genetic material we call deoxyribonucleic acid, or DNA, recovered from victims, weapons, crime scenes, and a multiplicity of items to the person of origin. The DNA examiner works every type of crime, breaking and enterings, sexual assaults, homicides, and any crime where there might be an exchange or deposition of trace genetic material. This examiner can recover DNA from the saliva deposited on the back of a stamp on a threatening letter or a cigarette butt left at a scene, or from sweat inside a hat or shirt. If there is cellular material on a surface, this examiner will find it and test it. The resolution of sexual assault investigations has been revolutionary, with the ability to match a single rapist to a multiplicity of assaults. By entering DNA data into a felon data bank, DNA examiners can identify persons who are recidivist criminals.

The DNA identity work of this examiner has enabled old "cold" cases to be solved and has resulted in the release of persons unjustly convicted of crimes where biologic material was recovered and can be retested with this exciting technology. The DNA examiner works with the forensic pathologist to perform family pedigrees to establish a kinship that will identify an unidentified decedent or match back fragments of a victim. This scientist is the innocent defendant's best friend by being able, with scientific certainty, to eliminate a person as the donor of biologic material recovered at a crime scene or on a murder victim. This discipline is at the forensic frontier with new information being discovered so quickly that scientific journals cannot keep pace. The forensic biologist is a forensic pioneer.

Forensic Microscopist

The forensic microscopist is the trace evidence person. Given fragments of paint from the clothes of a hit-and-run victim, the microscopist will give you the make and model of the offending vehicle. Find some hairs? The hair examiner can tell much from hairs' general characteristics, such as race, damage by coloring, and if it is in fact human. Sometimes criminals will passively transfer their pet's hair from crime scene to crime scene, telling the investigator to look for a criminal who spends time with animals. This scientist will tell you if material is animal, vegetable, or mineral. The forensic pathologist looks diligently on victims of violence to find trace evidence such as fibers from clothing or carpets to give to this scientist. Unknown materials often go first to this scientist for identification before being analyzed or referred to others for further analysis. The resolution of the Wayne Williams serial homicides of young black males in Atlanta represents a triumph of the forensic microscopist's study of carpet fibers, matching them back to carpet in the assailant's home and vehicles.

There are also many jobs in criminal investigation, working with police in local, state, or federal government, as well as in private companies in the insurance and financial industries. You'll find some examples of these jobs in this book.

How To Use This Book

As you read each woman's story, you'll find a checklist with some clues about what type of person would be good in the particular area profiled. You'll get ideas of what a typical day is like and what makes the hard work worthwhile. There is information about what salary you might expect to earn as you start out and as you grow.

The final chapter, Getting Started on Your Own Career Path, gives you some advice from the women on what to do now. You'll find recommendations on books to read, some recommended Web sites, and a list of organizations to contact for information about student programs and scholarships.

COOL careers

for girls

as

Crime Solvers

Louise Walzer

Louise Walzer

Criminalist and Assistant Director, Jefferson Parish Sheriff's Office, Jefferson Parish, Louisiana

Major in Biology and minor in Chemistry

Firearms
Examiner

Sure Shot on Crime

Louise Walzer often spends a good part of her day looking through a microscope at the patterns of microscopic markings (striations) on fired bullets and fired cartridge cases. Louise is responsible for examining firearms material involved in crimes in Jefferson Parish, Louisiana. She also receives cases from surrounding parishes. Louise uses scientific methods to try to answer these types of questions: Was a bullet fired from a certain gun? What type of gun fired a certain bullet or fired cartridge case found at a crime scene? How far was the gun from the victim when it was fired? Was the gun discovered at a crime scene used in other crimes as well?

When detectives and crime scene investigators find evidence of firearms—guns, bullets, fired cartridge cases, and other types of ammunition—they send

Firearms Examiner
Depends on years of experience and cost of living in the area. In Metairie, Louisiana, beginning salary is about $26,000 per year with good benefits and a company car. With time, salary can top out in the $40,000 range.

LOUISE'S CAREER PATH

Enjoys playing
▼ cowboys

Part-time lab technician,
▼ drug section, sheriff's
office crime lab

Interested in
▼ shooting
competitions

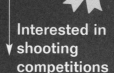

this material to the crime lab. The firearms material is logged in and eventually forwarded to Louise for examination. Louise tries to get as much information about the guns and ammunition to the detectives working the case as quickly as possible so they can apprehend the criminals. The sooner she can get the information to the detectives, the more likely it is that detectives will be able to solve the case.

Sometimes this race against time makes the job stressful because homicides can come in waves, and she will have a number of cases to work on at the same time. Naturally, all the lead detectives want their case worked first. The evidence remains in the place where it is logged in until Louise or her coworker, Tim Scanlan, is ready to examine it. Louise only takes one case at a time so evidence from one case is not mixed up with evidence from another.

Matching Bullets and Fired Cartridge Cases

Fired bullets have striations, or microscopic marks, located on the surface of the bullet. These striations are transferred to the bullet as it travels down the barrel. Fired cartridge cases have striations and compression marks produced when the firing pin strikes the primer. A gun that police suspect was used in a crime is test fired into a water tank (which not only stops the bullet but also protects it and allows Louise to retrieve it with the markings intact). The weapon is test fired three times.

The bullets and fired cartridge cases obtained are called reference

Graduates high
school in Florida

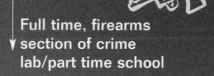
Full time, firearms
section of crime
lab/part time school

Becomes
Criminalist I

material and are used to compare to evidence bullets and fired cartridge cases. Louise uses a comparison microscope that allows her to see two images at one time. The evidence bullets or fired cartridge cases are placed on the left side, and the reference bullets feeling of accomplishment when a match is made," Louise says. "We use the buddy system in our laboratory. If I find a possible match, I will ask my coworker to check it and vice versa. If a match is made, we write careful notes, take Polaroid pictures

Research is 50 percent of the job.

I have to stay up on the latest weapons and

ammunition manufactured. In addition, there

are always new techniques for firearm analysis.

or fired cartridge cases are placed on the right side.

Examination can take five minutes or five days. "We get a wonderful to help refresh our memory when the case goes to court (often one or two years later), make official reports, and notify detectives."

13

LOUISE'S CAREER PATH

Trains at FBI
Academy/lectures
on firearms

President, Association
of Firearms and Tool
Mark Examiners

There are cases where only fired bullets and fired cartridge cases are obtained from a crime scene. No gun is found. In this case, Louise can examine these items and give the detectives a list of possible weapons.

Loves Research

When she isn't test firing a gun or looking into a microscope, Louise can be doing research, which is one of the things she likes best about her job. She uses the Internet, a computer database maintained by the FBI (Federal Bureau of Investigation), or a book from her firearms library. "We are now seeing ammunition and weapons that are manufactured in different countries all around the world."

The FBI and ATF (Alcohol, Tobacco, and Firearms) have joined together to provide a database system so firearms examiners across the nation can enter digital images of fired bullets and fired cartridge cases retrieved from crime scenes. This system can link several crimes committed by a single individual. The information helps detectives locate and apprehend criminals.

Testifying In Court

Louise is often asked to testify in court, sometimes many times in the same month. She will spend hours researching her notes, photographs, and background information on the ammunition and the weapons used in the case. In her 21 years of testifying, she has learned that if she does not make her testimony interesting, some jurors certainly will go to sleep. She now brings colorful posters of fired bullets with striations, the comparison microscope, and other "teaching" material with her to court.

Louise has a good relationship with many of the defense attorneys outside the courtroom. But in the courtroom, their job is to make her look incompetent in front of the jury. The prosecutors, or assistant district attorneys, sometimes expect too much from her. She realized years ago that these attorneys, both defense and prosecutors, are just doing their jobs and no matter who asks her a question, the answer will always be the same. "Testifying can be scary at times, but that's good because it keeps me on my toes." There are a few attorneys who try to intimidate her by getting right up in her face. Louise will take her glasses off and wipe them. This technique is subtle but it stops the attorneys from acting unprofessional.

There is nothing routine about Louise's job. She is always doing something new. She enjoys her job and looks forward to going to work in the morning.

CAREER CHECKLIST

You'll like this job if you ...

Love science

Like to take things apart and see how they work

Can be very safety-conscious

Like explaining complicated things to different types of people

Like to do research

Can deal with death and suffering

Have very good sense of spatial relationships

Are good at puzzles

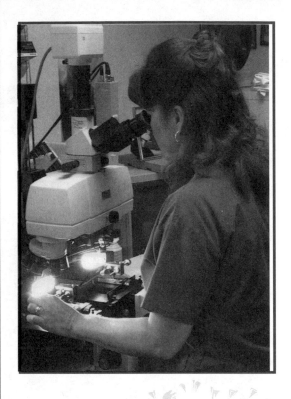

Always a Rebel

As a girl Louise was fascinated with what made things work and took apart several of the family's clocks, to the chagrin of her father. She loved to play cowboys with the neighborhood boys. "I am rebellious and have always liked doing things other people thought I shouldn't."

Her father, a news director for a local radio station, would have liked his younger of two daughters to be interested in more feminine careers, but Louise had her own ideas. At 18 she had decided she wanted to be a social worker with the police and work with delinquent girls. Her father knew the sheriff in Jefferson Parish and asked him how he could steer his daughter in another direction. The sheriff said Jefferson Parish was opening a new crime lab and that it would be a safer type of work, but might fulfill Louise's desire for "cloak and dagger" operations. Louise agreed to try it part time to see if she liked it. She also went to Loyola College part time and studied chemistry.

"In 1972 I was a laboratory technician in the drug analysis section. My duties included the analysis and identification of marijuana. Certain individuals of that era would store marijuana in plastic bags, travel, and not bathe. When these bags were seized and brought into the lab for analysis, they were often infested with body lice. That is when I started to reevaluate my current position in the laboratory."

When Louise's mentor and teacher moved over to firearms, she went with him. By this time Louise was working full time at the laboratory and attending St. Mary's Dominican College in New Orleans, where she studied biology, including two courses in microbiology and one course in parasitology. These courses helped her master the microscope and learn to identify unknowns.

She married a policeman, who also attended St. Mary's Dominican College. Her interest in police work and weapons grew. She shot in competitions until the birth of her son. When she got pregnant, she stopped competing and has not been involved since, except to test fire weapons at work.

Louise trained in firearms with her mentor for three years before finishing her degree. In 1979, after earning her Bachelor of Science degree, she became a Criminalist I, which meant she could examine cases on her own and testify to her findings in court. Since that time she has trained a number of assistants, the same way her mentor trained her.

"I told the last trainee, who is now a Criminalist I, one of the ways you will know when you are close to being ready is when you walk into a doctor's office, sit down, and, while waiting, start studying the repeatable patterns in the wallpaper. The examiner has to be able to recognize repeatable patterns or microscopic marks left on the evidence and match them to a suspect weapon."

Louise received training at the FBI Academy in Quantico, Virginia and has lectured to police from the Sheriff's Office in Jefferson Parish, as well as in surrounding parishes and at the FBI Academy. She feels the more detectives know about her work the better they will be at preserving important evidence at crime scenes. She's also lectured at colleges in her area.

Louise was president of the Louisiana Association of Forensic Scientists in 1985 and the first woman president of the Association of Firearms and Tool Mark Examiners in 1992, after holding several committee and officer positions in that international organization. Most of the members of the association are men.

It took extra effort to gain their respect and trust.

Kids and Husband Give Her Balance

Louise had two children with her first husband. They later divorced. Not long after that she met and married an engineer and architect, who is great with her kids and gives her balance in her life. "In this field of work, you learn to block yourself away from things you see at work; you cannot feel for the victims. There was one time when an assistant district attorney introduced me to the victim's family on a case I was ready to testify on. My guard was down and I became queasy because it then became personal." As a forensic scientist, Louise must always remain objective. "When I do testify in court, I create my own little world. The only people I focus on are the attorneys, judge, and jury; no one else exists. When I am not at work, I stay in touch with the real world. My husband and children help me to do that."

Louise has found other ways to stay in touch with the gentle side of life and forget about homicides, suicides, and

Forensic firearms examination is the combination of skill and science. It is science because we make scientific observations, conduct tests, and form our conclusions based on the results of these scientific tests. It is an art because opinions are based partly on subjectivity. Science is an organized body of knowledge; art is interpretative and does not adhere to a set of rules.

other violent crimes. In her spare time, she grows bonsai trees and works in her gardens. She also rehabilitates orphaned squirrels. Her husband built release cages for her. Eventually, she turns the squirrels loose to live in the wild again. She has rehabilitated 52 squirrels and is training others to help her. She is seriously considering working with a rehabilitation center after she retires from the crime laboratory in a few years.

Annie Carver–Jones

Annie Carver–Jones

Latent Fingerprint Examiner, Forensic Scientist, Latent Print Examiner, Northern Laboratory, Virginia Division of Forensic Science, Commonwealth of Virginia.

Major in Government Management

Latent Fingerprint
Examiner

ID Expert

Whether she's working with material such as plastic bags, sticky tape, glass, paper, weapons or even dead bodies, Annie Carver-Jones is usually helping identify someone. If there is a record of an individual's fingerprints in the Virginia Automated Fingerprint Identification System (AFIS) database and latent prints "lifted" from a crime scene match the prints in the database, Annie can say with certainty that a person visited a crime scene (although she can't say when). She also can identify a deceased person by taking the person's fingerprints.

Fingerprints are the most positive means of identifying individuals. Fingerprints are a reproduction of friction skin ridges found on the palm side of the hands and fingers. Similar friction skin can also be found on the

Latent Fingerprint Examiner
Forensic scientist trainees earn between $28,000 and $58,000 per year and forensic scientists from $37,000 to $76,000 per year in Virginia.

ANNIE'S CAREER PATH

▼ Receives cosmetology license, works as hair stylist	▼ Moves to Brooklyn, tests hair care products	▼ Moves to Washington, D.C. to be with family

surface of the palms and soles of the feet. No two individuals have the same fingerprints. Fingerprints are permanent and individually unique. Every finger bears a ridge arrangement that begins to form during fetal life and remains unchanged until decomposition of the body.

Annie is one of three examiners in the Latent Print Section of the Northern Virginia Forensic Laboratory. Together she and her colleagues are responsible for examining and processing items of evidence for latent prints when they are submitted in conjunction with other laboratory examinations. In addition, photographs, negatives, and "lifts" are scrutinized for identification purposes. Photographs of latent prints of value are always retained in the laboratory files and are available for future compar-

isons. The forensic laboratory assists 13 counties in the Northern Virginia region. Requests for laboratory examinations are submitted by police departments, sheriff's offices, fire marshal's offices, and other law enforcement agencies.

Works With All Types of Evidence

"We receive all types of evidence into the laboratory to be examined and processed for latent prints. Once an officer submitted a bi-fold door and I was able to recover the suspect's palm print. The suspect was hiding inside the closet and attacked the woman when she returned home."

For her cases, Annie determines the best method used to develop latent prints. The physical and chemical com-

Works in
▼ local hospital as
telephone operator

Meets and
▼ marries George

Joins FBI as
▼ fingerprint clerk

position of each item to be examined is considered when selecting the most appropriate method. The methods used to locate and develop latent prints generally fall in the following categories:

Powders – There are three reasons for using fingerprint powder to develop latent prints: 1) to make the print visible; 2) to develop contrast for photographic and/or comparison purposes; and 3) for lifting and preserving. Annie will select a powder that offers contrast to the surface on which the print is made. For example, she'll use black powder on light color surfaces and silver or gray powder on dark color surfaces.

Chemicals – Porous or absorbent surfaces such as paper, cardboard, or unfinished wood are processed chemically. Among the most commonly used are iodine, ninhydrin, and silver nitrate. For non-porous or non-absorbent surfaces, such as plastic, glass, metal, or glossy paper, Annie may use cyanoacrylate fuming, or "superglue." Development occurs when the fumes from the drying glue adhere to the latent print, usually producing a gray or white print.

Light Sources (laser detection) – In this process, laser light is absorbed by the sweat compound left on a surface. By use of filters, light from the latent fingerprint becomes visible and is photographed by a camera.

"Very seldom do we go to a crime scene," Annie says. "Most police departments have trained field evidence technicians to conduct the search for physical evidence at the crime scene. They have the equipment and skill to photograph the scene and examine it for the presence

ANNIE'S CAREER PATH

Metropolitan Police
Department, Washington,
D.C. fingerprint examiner

Moves to Northern
Virginia Forensic
Laboratory

of fingerprints, footprints, blood-stains, or any other type of evidence that may be relevant to the crime. However, I was asked to assist in printing the footprints of an abandoned 3-month old infant. The investigator wanted me to compare the footprints that I took with the footprints on file at the hospital. The

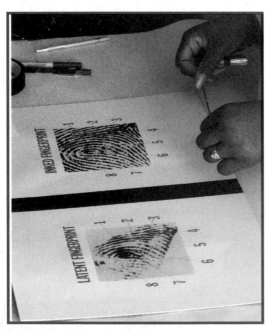

footprints were compared and found to be one and the same (a match)."

The search for physical evidence at a crime scene must be thorough and systematic. Where to search and what to search for will be determined by the circumstances of the crime. For example, in the case of homicides, the search will be centered on the weapon and any evidence left as a result of contact between victim and assailant. For a burglary the point of entry must be established and then examined for toolmarks, fingerprints, etc. In the case of a deceased victim, the body is transported to the medical examiner's office to determine cause of death and obtain such items as clothing, fingerprints, fingernail scrapings, blood, head, and pubic hairs.

"The physical evidence collected must be handled and processed in a way to prevent any changes from taking place between the time it is removed from the crime scene and the time it is submitted to the laboratory. Some changes may occur, such as contamination, breakage, evaporation, or careless packaging."

Annie will work the oldest cases in the laboratory first unless there is an "Urgent" case, which will take priority.

Her cases can take as little as an hour or as long as several months, depending on the amount of evidence submitted in a particular case.

Annie has testified numerous times in federal, state, and local courts. "I am subpoenaed to appear in court practically every month. Sometimes the case doesn't go to trial because the person confesses when confronted with the evidence."

Annie says the most challenging cases are the ones that involve homicides, especially when it's a child. The most satisfying thing is being able to bring closure to a family, whether it's identifying a loved one in a homicide case, a major disaster, or the perpetrator who burglarized a home or business.

CAREER CHECKLIST ✓

You'll like this job if you ...

- Have lots of patience to examine fine detail

- Have a good visual sense

- Are organized and orderly

- Can communicate and work harmoniously with others using discretion and tact

- Can make convincing presentations

- Will take all appropriate safety and security precautions

- Love to learn and will keep learning your entire life

First Works as Hair Stylist

Annie grew up in Fayetteville, North Carolina, one of four children. After high school, she enrolled in DeShazor's School of Beauty Culture. She received her cosmetology license and worked one year in a hair salon as a hair stylist. At the age of 20 she left home for New York, where friends were living, and found a job in the research department of a company testing hair care products. When the company closed, she began employment with Bell Telephone Company. Police officers who had the particular "beat" where she was working would come into the building for a "security check" and to talk. She was interested in the stories they told about their work.

Annie's mother worried about her daughter being in such a big city and finally, after six years, Annie moved to Washington, DC, where a sister and brother lived. She got a job as a telephone operator at a local hospital and met the man she later married, George, who also worked at the hospital.

"I had a friend who was working with the FBI, and she informed me they had recruiters who were looking for people to join the agency. I applied and fortunately I was accepted. I received my basic training in fingerprint identification at the FBI. This training included the Henry System of fingerprint classifications and procedures. I performed classifying, searching, sequencing, and filing fingerprint cards to ascertain an arrestee's true name and criminal status."

After three years, Annie joined the Washington, D.C. Metropolitan Police Department. She continued to work as a fingerprint examiner. Later, Annie was accepted into the Latent Print Trainee Program. She received one year of extensive training in the field of latent print identification. This training included the development, preservation, and comparison of latent prints, obtaining prints from unknown deceased and sometimes badly decomposed individuals, as well as the preparation of courtroom testimony.

"When I decided to leave the FBI it was for a career change. I knew I had a better chance of obtaining my goal—working in the Latent Print Section—and an increase in salary. As a latent print examiner, the work is exciting and more rewarding. You communicate directly with attorneys and law enforcement personnel in order to provide information about evidence recovery, to receive information about specific cases, and to prepare for court testimony."

Annie worked with the D.C. Police Department for ten years before accepting a position with the Northern Virginia Forensic Laboratory. She examines physical evidence recovered at crime scenes in order to determine whether latent prints are present, prepares reports and exhibits for court defending analysis, and testifies as an expert witness. Also, Annie is responsible for training law enforcement personnel in the recognition, collection, and preservation of evidence.

Annie is very involved in her church. She also likes to sew and to read, and she does arts and crafts and enjoys the theatre.

GROUNDBREAKERS
High Tech Detective

Michelle Buchanan worked for many years as an analytical chemist at the Oak Ridge National Laboratory. She specialized in mass spectrometry—a technology that detects minute traces of anything from pollutants in air to toxins in food by reading the characteristic signatures of individual compounds. Buchanan and her colleagues conducted a study to understand why children's fingerprints disappear faster than adult fingerprints. She found that children's fingerprints contain more volatile chemicals, while adult prints display longer lasting, higher molecular weight compounds.

Source: "Pioneer Women: Pushing the Frontiers of Science and Engineer at Oak Ridge National Laboratory," *SIRS Government Reporter*, 1995.

Mary Manhein

Mary Manhein

Director, Louisiana State University Forensic Anthropology Laboratory and Forensic Anthropology and Computer Enhancement Services (FACES)

Major in English, MA in Anthropology, Louisiana State University

Forensic Anthropologist

The Bone Lady

"If you don't mind low pay, night and weekend work, treacherous recovery sites, snakes, mosquitoes, and poison ivy, then a career in forensic anthropology and bio-archaeology could give you amazing job satisfaction," says Mary Manhein. Mary excavates and studies the bones of recently or long deceased individuals. She can help police determine the identity of the person whose bones have been found, or how that person died. The bones and other material found with them give her the clues.

Mary gets about 40 cases a year from police all over the country who need the help of her forensic anthropology laboratory at Louisiana State University. When bones arrive in her laboratory, Mary and her two research associates and the various graduate students who work with her

Forensic Anthropolgist
Many forensic anthropologists begin as part-time instructors where the salaries are very low. Some students actually start teaching in night school and work another job during the day. For full-time work, salaries range between $35,000 and $55,000 per year.

remove any soft tissue from the skeleton before they begin to build their profile of age, sex, and race.

By measuring the bones and examining their configuration, forensic anthropologists usually can tell whether the deceased person was a male or female (the hip bones are different, for one thing) and about how old the person was at death (this is often apparent from the hip bone also). They can

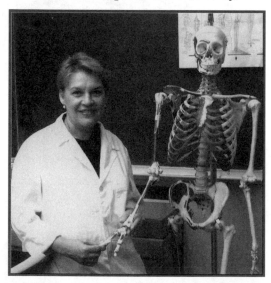

tell the person's race by the configuration of the skull. Sometimes they can tell that the person died a violent death; for example, when there is a suspicious perimortem break—a break that occurs at or near the time of death. Often x-rays of the skull or other bones will reveal tiny bits of metal that may be fragments of bullets. Coupled with a hole in a bone that is probably an entry or exit wound for a bullet, this is good evidence that the person died from gunshot wounds.

Often the loved ones of a deceased person whose remains have been hidden by a killer will keep hoping that their family member is still alive. Mary can help identify bones and help the relatives at least know what happened to the missing person. "I think of a mother out there somewhere or

MA degree
▼ from LSU

Takes over
▼ forensic lab

Builds lab's
▼ reputation

another family member wanting to know where that person is, what happened to their loved one. That's what pushes me a lot. It's rewarding being able to bring justice for those people who cannot speak for themselves. I cannot bear it that we have cases in our laboratory that remain unidentified. I don't lose sleep over it, I'm not obsessed with it, but I do want these individuals to go home. They don't belong in a box in our lab. They belong at home. And women, I think, especially identify with that, because they are in tune with others and have sympathy for them."

Historic Forensic Anthropology

Mary also excavates and examines very old bones. Often she is called upon to help excavate newly found graves that could be 100 years old or more. Recently, for example, Mary and some of her students worked with remains of French soldiers from the early 1700s that were found in Mississippi along the Mississippi River bank when the Corps of Engineers worked to shore up the bank. "We know the French were in the area in the early 1700s and we know they are French soldiers because French soldiers wore uniform pants with four little buttons in a square called the French fly, and these buttons were in the graves— everything had deteriorated, almost, except the buttons and the teeth. These graves are the earliest of any historic burials that we have in this entire region so we were so excited to be asked to participate in this."

Mary is one of the world's experts

on historic coffins. She has excavated skeletons from three centuries and has researched how coffins were made in different periods. "One of the French soldiers must have been a giant. They built the coffins to fit and the coffin is more than six feet long."

Other Responsibilities

In addition to her responsibilities running the forensic anthropology lab, Mary teaches anthropology and advises undergraduate anthropology students. She also is an advisor to about 15 graduate students, and must help them plan their projects and review their theses. "There are people from all over the place wanting to come here to school to work with me, but I've had to turn down many students this year, because I just don't have the time anymore. I teach 25 percent of the time, forensics is about 50 percent of my time, and research is another 25 percent."

Mary also gives talks to groups all over the United States about the work done in her laboratory. "It's good PR for both the laboratory and me. I like the idea of maintaining the stability of our reputation within the community."

We recently recovered some historic remains of French soldiers from the early 1700s.

One of Ten Children

As a child, Mary's family of farmers moved frequently between southwest Arkansas and northwest Louisiana. She was one of ten children and her family was very poor. One of her most vivid memories is losing a little brother to death. She says that is part of the reason she became a forensic anthropologist. But Mary has some wonderful memories from her childhood as well, like spending hours in front of the fireplace listening to relatives tell stories. She especially liked the stories of her mother and her Aunt Penny. Being a storyteller is natural to her and has helped her in her teaching and, more recently, in writing books.

Mary loved school. She was an avid reader and got excellent grades. After high school she wondered what she would do with her life. She didn't realize she could go to college even though her family was poor. She probably would have been able to get a scholarship if someone had advised her on how to apply, but no one told her she could do that. The summer

CAREER CHECKLIST ✓

You'll like this job if you ...

Love science

Have lots of patience

Like to do puzzles and solve mysteries

Have a genuine sympathy for others and want to help people who have lost loved ones

Have lots of energy and will be able to juggle many different types of responsibilities

Would be a good teacher, like to explain things to others

Will find creative ways to get the money needed to run a lab

home mom until my second child, the second boy, went to kindergarten. I had taken one night course at a local university just before I married and aced it, so I knew I would be a good student. I was eager to start college."

College Later in Life

Mary entered school at Louisiana State University in Baton Rouge in her early thirties. She majored in English, which she had done very well with in her high school studies. From then on her life was juggling kids and school. Most of the responsibilities of raising her children fell on Mary because her husband traveled so much in his job. "I really wanted my children to have a good childhood so I arranged my school work around their schedule. They always came first. The fact that they turned out to be outstanding young men tells me I did it right. Bill was also a very good father."

In her senior year in college, at age 37, Mary took a course called Old World Archaeology and fell in love with anthropology. She had just about

after graduation a business school did offer her some help with tuition. She began her career that fall studying at business school while she worked part time to pay for part of the tuition. Then she worked as a secretary in a personnel department for several years.

"I liked it but I really wanted to do something important with my life. I always felt that I would. I fell in love with Bill and ultimately left that job. We got married and I had a child. Bill, who was in sales, got transferred to southern Louisiana. I was a stay-at-

decided to get another undergraduate degree in anthropology when she learned that she could go straight into the graduate program without having to take the undergraduate courses first. "So I started the master's program in anthropology. All during my graduate studies I either volunteered or had a graduate assistantship in the anthropology department. Halfway into my first year of graduate school I reviewed the four sub-disciplines of anthropology: archaeology, cultural anthropology, linguistic anthropology, and physical anthropology. I decided to combine archaeology and physical anthropology into what was then becoming known by some as the fifth sub-discipline—applied anthropology, in my case forensic anthropology.

"I had met Dr. Doug Owsley, who worked on bones at LSU. I started volunteering in his lab, fell in love with it, and when he left I started running the lab. I began as a part-time instructor and just wouldn't leave. I talked the department head into hiring me part time because I loved to teach and wanted to share

GROUNDBREAKERS
Pioneer in Bone Studies

Mildred Trotter, born in 1899, received a fellowship to study physical anthropology at Oxford in 1926. She was the first woman to obtain a full professorship at Washington University Medical School in St. Louis.

Trotter was an anatomist and physical anthropologist whose pioneering bone studies contributed to a wide range of disciplines, including forensic science. Her method of using the length of certain bones to estimate the height of their owners in life has been a primary tool of forensic experts and physical anthropologists since its formulation in 1952.

Trotter also served as the director of the Central Identification Laboratory in Oahu, Hawaii, where she identified skeletal remains of war dead found in the Pacific. When she moved to Washington University Medical School, St. Louis detectives regularly consulted her about unidentified bones.

Source: *Notable Twentieth Century Scientists*, Gale Research, 1995

the joys of anthropology with students. I have taught thousands and thousands of students."

Building a World Famous Lab

Mary built the forensic anthropology lab into the world-famous laboratory it is today. "The cases continued to come in. It was a small lab then and we had only one room, but as I began to do workshops for law enforcement people, our laboratory grew both in size and number of cases, and also in recognition not only in Louisiana but also throughout the world. We did the traditional forensic anthropology work at first, and then we added computer enhancements, we did age progressions, and now we do clay facial reconstructions as well."

The LSU forensic lab is unique in the United States because of all of these special types of work offered in one laboratory. Eileen Barrow, the research associate who does the facial reconstruction at LSU's FACES (Forensic Anthropology and Computer Enhancement Services) lab, can take a skull and glue tissue depth markers to it that indicate where the soft tissue of the face normally would be. Then she uses clay to "rebuild" the person's face. Many times this is the last chance the police will have to identify a person's remains. At the lab, Mary and her assistants also use software to age-progress children and adults who are missing. In addition, they have software that aids in cleaning up or enhancing blurred videotapes that can help to identify robbers caught in the act of holding up a store.

Education Gave Her Confidence

Mary never felt like she was in control of her life until she started college. "Once I began to get an education, I gained confidence. I'm doing exactly what I want to do now; there is not one other thing I would rather be doing. I have found where I belong. That takes knowing who you are and accepting it. We can't change the past but we have a lot to do with where we

I think of a mother out there somewhere

or another family member

wanting to know where that person is,

what happened to their family member.

That's what drives me.

are going. There is nothing I can't do if I set my mind to it."

In 1999 Mary received East Baton Rouge Parish's YWCA award for Woman of the Year in the area of public service. "I had never been so humbled in my life as I was when I got that award. I cried, and it's hard to make me cry."

When she isn't working in the lab or traveling to get publicity for the university, these days Mary probably is working on a book. She wrote about her work in her book *The Bone Lady,* published by LSU Press in 1999. *Softly They Die* is her first mystery.

The protagonist is, of course, a forensic anthropologist. Mary gets up early in the morning to do her writing, when the only "people" awake to keep her company are her cat Maggie and her dog Bogey.

Juliann F. Willey

Juliann F. Willey

Forensic Microscopist and Crime Laboratory Director, the Delaware State Police

Major in Biology and Genetic Engineering Technology, minor in Chemistry

Forensic
Microscopist

Detective With a Microscope

Juliann Willey is the only forensic microscopist in the state of Delaware. She is employed by the Delaware State Police. "I analyze hairs and fibers taken from the scene of a crime and compare those to known hairs and fibers from the suspect and victim to answer questions like where the crime took place, what instrument was used, and whether two people came in contact with each other."

If someone has been killed or beaten, crime scene investigators from the local or state police will send Julie samples of hair found on a weapon (like a baseball bat or car) or other object. They also will send her a known hair sample from the victim. When the police have a suspect they think may have committed the crime, Julie will receive a sample of that person's hair, too. One of her jobs is to compare those

Forensic Microscopist
Can earn $30,000 or more right out of college. Salary progresses with years of services.

JULIE'S CAREER PATH

Studies genetic
engineering at
Cedar Crest College

Work for DuPont
as research
chemist

Forensic Chemist,
Office of Medical
Examiner

hairs found at the crime scene with the known hair samples from the victim and the suspect. She does this using a comparison microscope (two microscopes connected with an optically perfect bridge so she can see both the crime scene samples and known samples at the same time).

"I could say in my report that the crime scene sample questioned item is consistent with the known hairs of the victim or suspect. I would not be able to say for sure that the hairs found at the crime scene came from a specific person, as you could do with DNA analysis. Generally I will get cases where DNA analysis is inconclusive or where there is no DNA present at the crime scene. For example, if a person committing a robbery had a ski mask that he pulled off and discarded in an alley, investigators would bring me that ski mask to collect any hairs that might be present."

Julie looks for hairs and fibers that previously have gone unnoticed when she examines material brought to her lab from the crime scene, such as clothing. She uses a high intensity lightsource and a microscope to look for the hairs and fibers that may provide clues about what happened. Sometimes the only physical evidence at a crime scene is found this way.

Examining Fiber

Microscopists examine fibers found on the body or at the crime scene to try to determine facts that will help the police catch the criminal, like where a crime took place. One of the main reasons Delaware has a microscopy laboratory is that a serial killer operating in the

Marries
▼ Dan

Sets up microscopy
▼ unit at Delaware State
Police crime lab

Has first son
▼ Danny

state was apprehended partly because of microscopy work. A man was killing women and discarding their bodies in different locations within the state. Some of the bodies had blue carpet fibers found on them. Because there was no microscopist in Delaware (this was before Julie started working there), the fibers were sent to an FBI laboratory for analysis. It turned out that the carpet fibers were from a type of carpet that was not made for very long because the fibers could not hold the dye that gave the carpet its color. The police were able to learn which stores had sold that type of carpet and who bought it. One of the people who bought the blue carpet had used it to customize a van. He subsequently sold that van to the individual who was later convicted as the serial killer. The victims had been in the killer's van at some point.

New Crime Lab Brought Her Opportunity

When the State Police in Delaware opened up a new crime laboratory, they added a microscopy unit because microscopy had played such an important part in the capture of the serial killer. Although sending the evidence to the FBI laboratory had proved effective in helping to solve the case of this serial killer, sometimes when the federal laboratories have lots of work, local investigators must wait a long time before they get the analysis on their crime scene materials. So Delaware decided it was better to do its own microscopy work when possible.

At the time Delaware announced it was building a new crime laboratory that would have a microscopist, Julie

JULIE'S CAREER PATH

Promoted to crime lab director

Has second son Joshua

was working in the only other state-run forensic laboratory in Delaware. This lab was the Office of the Chief Medical Examiner. Julie's job title was forensic chemist. She analyzed confiscated drugs to determine their composition. She also analyzed body fluids and tissue in questionable deaths to determine how much alcohol or drugs were in a person's system at the time of death.

Discovers Forensics

"When I was a senior in college, DNA was utilized for the first time in forensic science. My degree was in genetic engineering, which was very strong in DNA. I knew by this time I really wanted to work in this field of forensics. (I had started college with the idea of becoming a veterinarian but got interested in genetics when I started taking genetics courses.) I graduated from college in 1988 and the only crime lab that existed in the state of Delaware was the Office of the Chief Medical Examiner. It had no job openings. So I got a job as a researcher at DuPont (a large manufacturer of chemicals and other products based in Delaware)."

Julie worked at DuPont as a technician and research chemist for two

42

years. She worked with a group of people who did research using a virus to generate substances less expensively than chemically manufacturing them. She kept looking for a job in a crime laboratory and eventually landed the job in the Chief Medical Examiner's Office.

Julie applied for the job of microscopist at the new crime laboratory when she saw they were building the new laboratory and got it because of her previous forensic experience. The state sent her for microscopy training at the FBI Academy in Quantico, Virginia and at the McCrone Research Institute in Chicago, Illinois. She was responsible for setting up the microscopy laboratory for the new crime lab. "It was an interesting challenge. I treated it like a big research project. I had to find out what type of equipment I needed. I talked to other people who ran these labs throughout the country."

Julie worked as a microscopist for two years, during 1992 and 1993. She was one of five civilian employees at the Delaware State Police crime lab. In 1993 the state decided it would be good to have a civilian director to head the

CAREER CHECKLIST ✓

You'll like this job if you ...

- Are extremely organized/can manage your time well

- Enjoy science, especially biology and chemistry

- Can communicate and work well with all different types of people

- Are curious about genetics and why you inherit certain characteristics

- Like detail work and are very patient

- Enjoy writing/can communicate well in both written and spoken word

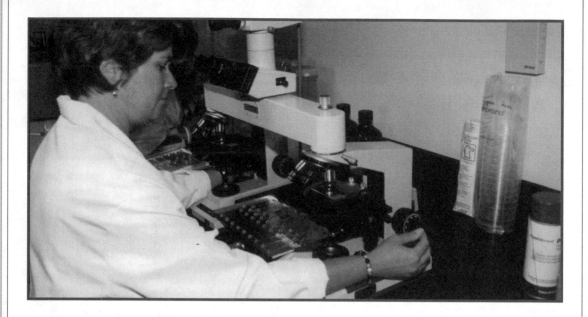

crime lab instead of the police officer previously used. Julie was awarded the position, even though she had been with the laboratory for the shortest amount of time of any of the civilians.

"It was kind of tough going at first. All of a sudden I had much more responsibility and I was the new kid on the block. I was fiscally responsible for the laboratory as well as other training units. I was responsible for making sure people got the equipment and supplies they needed. I had to research how to get the right equipment and the best prices from the vendors who supply the laboratory. Also, when I was promoted to director I had my five-

month old baby Danny at home." Julie had met her husband Dan in 1989 and they got married two years later. The two met at a party in Wilmington, Delaware, where they discovered they had friends in common. Dan is a computer crime specialist with the Delaware State Police.

"The lab director part of my job takes 60 to 70 percent of my time, and the microscopy takes the rest. While scientific method and background, patience, and care are necessary in the microscopy part of my job, I need good organizational, time management, and interpersonal skills in my role as crime lab director. I also have to have good math skills and know-how to be very diplomatic, because part of my job is reconciling how we spend the money in our laboratory—who gets to buy what."

In 1997 Julie had another baby, Joshua. "My husband and I are probably overprotective of our kids, because we see some of the bad things that go on in the world." When she isn't working, Julie likes to play tennis, garden, and watch her boys play ice hockey and baseball.

Julie is on the board of the American Society of Crime Laboratory Directors and is a member of the American Academy of Forensic Science and the local division of the International Association for Identification. In 1996 she served as a role model for an advertising campaign called "Expect the Best From a Girl," where she encouraged girls in math and science. She went to New York to be filmed for a television advertisement and also prepared a radio ad and a print ad for newspapers and magazines. Recently, she had the pleasure of giving a commencement speech to her alma mater, Cedar Crest College in Allentown, Pennsylvania.

GROUNDBREAKERS
Geneticist

Barbara McClintock, born in 1902, was one of the most influential geneticists of the 20th century. Her revolutionary work on gene and chromosome behavior has come to be acknowledged as a fundamental concept of gene functioning.

McClintock was one of a few scientists who early developed an understanding of chromosomes as a basis of heredity. She also discovered the nuclear organizer of the chromosome, a structure that serves to order genetic material during cell division.

She was elected to the National Academy of Sciences and was the first woman to become president of the Genetics Society of America. In 1983 she became the first woman to win a Nobel Prize in physiology and medicine.

Source: *The 100 Most Influential Women of All Time*, Deborah G. Felder.

Celeste Dodson

Celeste Dodson

Section Manager, Auto/Fire Special Investigative Unit, State Farm Insurance, Columbia, Maryland

Major in Criminology, Fraud Claim Law Specialist designation

Investigator—
Insurance Fraud

Fraud Fighter

Celeste Dodson was interested in investigation and law enforcement from the time she was a kid. Her parents and other relatives thought she would outgrow her interest, and they discouraged her from a career as a policewoman or an FBI agent because they thought law enforcement was a dangerous profession for a woman. But Celeste didn't lose interest. Although others tried to convince her to study something else, she chose to major in criminology in college, and she chose her college—Florida State University—because it had an excellent reputation for criminology studies.

"As a child I liked figuring out any kind of mystery. Also, I never liked people telling me what I could and couldn't do. When I was in high school my parents paid for some aptitude tests for me to help me decide what career to

Investigator

Insurance claim representatives start at the mid $30,000 range. Can earn $60,000 to $70,000 at mid-career and more than $100,000 as a top manager.

CELESTE'S CAREER PATH

Intern, Florida
State Attorney's
Office

BS degree,
Criminology,
Florida State U

Private
Investigator

prepare for. The tests said I should be an investigator. So when people told me to think of another career, I would just say 'This is what I know I will be good at; this is what I want to do. I believe strongly in fighting crime'."

Celeste is glad she didn't let anyone dissuade her from studying criminology. Many of her parents' friends had jobs they didn't like and couldn't wait to leave at night. "I never wanted to be like that. I wanted to have a job that I would look forward to every morning and hate to leave at night and that I was just really excited about. My job is like that."

Celeste manages the special investigative unit (SIU) for State Farm Insurance in Maryland, Delaware, Washington, D.C., and West Virginia. There are many different types of insurance fraud. Some insured individ-

uals intentionally burn their houses, crash their cars, stage theft losses, or claim injury when really no injury has occurred—all with the aim of collecting money that does not belong to them. All these actions are fraud and often they are crimes.

SIUs investigate insurance claims that are suspicious in nature. The SIU tries to resolve claims that are suspicious and find the truth. If the claims are valid, the SIU wants to see that they get paid as soon as possible. However, if the claims are not valid and the insured or claimant is committing insurance fraud, the SIU investigator will take the necessary steps to resist payment on the claim and refer the case to the appropriate authorities. Insurance claim fraud is serious and costly. "It's estimated that between 10 and 30 percent of all claims are fraud-

Auto/Home Owner
▼ Claim Rep, State
Farm

Joins State Farm
▼ Special Investigative
Unit (SIU)

Sets up SIU for
▼ eastern states

ulent and that the insurance industry pays at least $79 billion in fraudulent claims," Celeste says.

Many Responsibilities

As section manager for a region in the eastern United States, Celeste is responsible for managing 47 people—SIU claim representatives/investigators, supervisors, and clerical staff. She has to make sure that all the SIU investigators follow the company's procedures. She reviews all claims that investiga-

tors have said are fraudulent. She works with state insurance bureaus that are responsible for monitoring fraud to make sure they are getting the reports and other information they need about the trends in insurance fraud and what State Farm is doing to prevent fraud. She attends civil trials when the company has to take someone to court or respond to a court action from a plaintiff. She works with the authorities at their request, assisting them in their fight against insurance fraud. She also lobbies at the state lev-

It's estimated that between 10 and 30 percent of all insurance claims are fraudulent. The insurance industry pays $79 billion in fraudulent claims.

els for laws that will make it harder to commit insurance fraud.

One of Celeste's responsibilities is serving as the chair and president of the Maryland Anti-Car Theft Committee. "This committee was created at the request of the governor of Maryland to help law enforcement reduce vehicle theft. I joined as a representative of State Farm and because of my contacts with the law enforcement community. I've had opportunities to meet with the police chiefs of different counties, insurance commissioners, and regulators to help in the development of policies that will reduce theft." For example, Celeste is working in Washington, D.C. to get laws changed so that towing companies have to report where they tow cars that are illegally parked within a certain time frame.

This will make it easier for the public to locate their cars and less likely that cars will be reported, incorrectly, as stolen. "That's one thing I love about SIU. You look at the big picture. There are so many avenues you can follow to get involved."

Celeste was promoted to her present position after she had worked for six years in an SIU in Florida.

She grew up in College Park and Columbia, Maryland. When she moved back to the Maryland area, it was like coming home.

Sets Up the SIU

Celeste was recruited to start SIUs for the Maryland, Delaware, and Washington, D.C areas. "I organized the units, figured out the kind of people I wanted to hire, trained them, set up the parameters of what we would be doing, and got it going. I started out with 5 and now have 18 SIU claims representatives in Maryland, D.C., and Delaware. I also have 10 in West Virginia and I supervise clerical staff and managers."

To start the units, Celeste first asked people who worked in insurance in the area, law enforcement officials, and insurance bureau representatives what type of problems they were seeing with insurance claims in the area. "In some areas there were more problems with arson, in other areas there appeared to be more problems with thefts and more staged auto accidents. You have to

CAREER CHECKLIST ✓

You'll like this job if you ...

Have a strong sense of justice, want to find the truth

Are not easily intimidated, are tenacious

Like to solve puzzles and mysteries

Can work independently

Are good at interviewing people

Are practical and have lots of common sense

Can represent yourself well in front of a group

know your areas and what the problems are. Of course, any type of insurance fraud can occur anywhere."

Celeste looked for people who were analytical and detail oriented to work in the SIUs. She needed some employees who could filter through lots of data to find patterns so that State Farm could see if there were organized crime rings operating in her areas. She also looked for people who had drive, were persistent in getting information, and didn't need to be told what to do every step of the way. She wanted everyone she hired to believe that insurance fraud was wrong and to care about stopping it. Insurance fraud hurts everybody because it makes the rates for insurance higher for all policyholders.

Everyone Celeste hired had to have experience as a claims representative with State Farm. "I had law enforcement people contact me and say they were interested. I said 'great, but first get claims experience for a couple of years'."

Celeste sent her employees for training sponsored by State Farm's corporate offices. She also did some of her own training. "I put together information from different organizations that deal with insurance fraud and also a lot of case law on insurance fraud that I had gathered over the years. I wanted my employees to understand legally how to investigate a claim, if appropriate pay the customer, and if not, resist payment of the claim. I also sent them out to ride with other SIU investigators in different parts of the country.

"I continually reminded them to find the truth, whatever that truth was. As they took claims, initially I looked at every aspect of their case. As they proved their ability to investigate it properly, I backed off and gave them space.

"When I was given the opportunity to start my own units, there were not many SIUs. Unfortunately, over the years as fraud has grown, the trend to have more SIU investigators has grown as well. But when I set up the first unit, there weren't any State Farm SIU investigators in Maryland, so the company had to look outside the state for someone who was qualified. I was known nationally by the claims I had handled and the contacts I'd made. I came up and interviewed for the position and they hired me. I had interviewed for another position and was not selected, but this is the best job I could have had. I had some guidelines in setting up the units, but I was given a lot of freedom to set them up the way I wanted. It was like having a ball of play dough and being told, go out and build an effective way to fight fraud."

Her Investigator Experience

Celeste knew what was required to be a good SIU investigator because she had done it herself. In Florida she joined the SIU after working for almost two years as an auto claims representative and two years as a homeowner claim representative based in the Jacksonville area. Celeste joined State Farm knowing she wanted to work her way up into the SIU. "When I had been in auto claims for a year and one half, I decided I wanted to move to homeowner claims to be cross-trained. My goal was to eventually be an SIU claims rep and not be limited in the types of claims I could handle.

"I was told by many people, if you want to get to management, you shouldn't leave auto claims or it will take you longer. But I thought 'no, management isn't what I'm looking for. I want to be an investigator so I'm going to do what I need to do to prepare myself in the best possible way for that job.' When I became a claim representative in State Farm's Florida SIU they were doing primarily fire investigations, but I was able to help them grow in the area of auto investigations. Some people said 'If you want to get into management, don't go into SIU.' But it turns out they were wrong."

Celeste was an SIU claim representative/investigator for six years. She took suspicious claims referred by claims reps in auto and homeowner claims. The National Insurance Crime Bureau has guidelines on what claims should be considered suspicious. "For example, these could be things like the tax on a receipt doesn't add up or no physical evidence to indicate the car or house had been broken into. When a claim is sent to the SIU, our main goal is to resolve the issues and pay the claim.

"To do that we might investigate why the tax on the receipt doesn't add up to what it should be, for example. Did the store clerk make a mistake or was the receipt altered in some way? If a house burns down we will hire an expert to determine the cause of the fire. If the expert determines the fire was intentionally set, then we will interview the insured individuals to find out where they were and what type of property they had in the house. If they said there was a grand piano in the house and we didn't find any evidence of a grand piano in the remains of the fire (and you would find the metal frame of the piano), then we have questions. Any time there is a fire that has been deliberately set, we have to determine if the insured had any involvement. We would like to remove them from suspicion, and we do that by interviewing them, their neighbors, the fire fighters, the fire marshals, and anyone who might have been around when the fire started.

"An investigator does one thing always. We always attempt to interview the policyholder/insured. The insured will give us information that will lead us to other people, and we follow those leads. We may interview a neighbor and we follow those leads. We may interview a fire marshal and we follow those leads. We are trying to get the whole picture of what occurred. Oftentimes we find the insured clearly had no involvement and our investigation may lead us to somebody else.

"We're not out there to deny claims. We're out there to find the truth. As an SIU investigator you really have to dig. You have a few things that you must do, but you also have to follow your gut instincts. You are trying to find out who would be able to help resolve the problem. It's like putting the pieces of a puzzle together. You have to verify what people tell you."

As it is important to go where the investigation leads you, Celeste's investigations have led her to a variety of different locations. She has interviewed people at motorbiker bars, and has interviewed doctors and lawyers at their offices. On occasion she has dealt with people with emotional problems and criminal histories. "You have to deal with all types of people and you have to be good with people. I'm a people watcher. I'm intrigued by why people do the things they do. When you interview people as an investigator, you have to watch everything they do. You are looking for clues in their body movements, their eye motions, and any inconsistencies in what they say. But you have to understand that just because they aren't telling you the truth doesn't mean they are trying to perpetrate insurance fraud. They may not be telling you the truth for a number of reasons that have nothing to do with your case."

Leah Bush

Leah Bush

Assistant Chief Medical Examiner, Commonwealth of Virginia, Norfolk, VA

Double major in Biology and Psychology; MD, Medical College of Virginia, Richmond, VA; Forensic Pathology Fellowship, Medical College of Virginia

Forensic Pathologist

A Voice for the Victim

Every day is different and there are always surprises for Dr. Leah Bush. Leah is a pathologist and has been a medical examiner (ME) in Norfolk, Virginia for more than 12 years. A pathologist is a physician who studies and determines the origins and causes of disease and death. An ME answers questions about the way an individual whose death is suspect died by autopsying the body. In an autopsy, the ME is looking for clues that point to the cause and manner of death. Not every person who dies has an autopsy, but if the death is suspicious the ME will examine the body and internal organs to try to get answers to questions like these: Where did the person die? What caused the death? Was the death a crime? Within what time period did the person die?

Forensic Pathologist
Medical examiners fresh from a fellowship earn about $85,000 per year. Experienced, board-certified medical examiners can make about $120,000 per year.

LEAH'S CAREER PATH

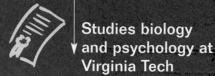

- Gets good grades throughout high school
- Studies biology and psychology at Virginia Tech
- Accepted to medical school

Sometimes the ME will find that the person died of an illness or disease; another person did not cause the death. But more frequently the information about how the person died will help the police catch a killer. For example, Leah might tell the police that a paring knife of a certain width, length, and thickness was used in a stabbing death. She could learn this by examining the stab wounds on the victim's body.

Leah works for the Commonwealth of Virginia. She is one of two MEs in the Tidewater District of the state. There are four crime laboratory regions in Virginia and MEs in each region. All the MEs report to the Chief Medical Examiner in Richmond, the state's capital. The regional MEs are responsible for running their own offices—hiring the people to work there,

making sure they use the resources the state gives them wisely and that they have the right equipment, dividing up the autopsy work, and supervising the doctors that go to the crime scenes when a murder may have been committed. MEs also have to testify in court about their findings.

"When we have subpoenas for court we have to stop what we are doing and just go. They tell us about what time they want us to be there, but sometimes we have to sit and wait until they call us," Leah says. "It's frustrating because we would rather be using the time we are just sitting and waiting to do our work." Leah might testify in court about the cause of death or about the type of wounds or bruises on the body.

"We have two permanent autopsy assistants and a couple of medical

58

Pathology resident
and part-time medical
examiner

Fellowship studying
under Virginia Chief
Medical Examiner

Gets married,
then divorced

students that get assigned to us each month. We teach the medical students how to do autopsies—how to draw diagrams of the body and dissect the organs. We also have a medico-legal death investigator. If a sudden death comes in and there is no medical history, I ask the investigator to call the family or the local physician to find out the person's history.

"We also have almost 50 physicians that work for us part time as deputy medical examiners. They are doctors licensed to practice medicine in the Commonwealth of Virginia (MDs but not usually pathologists). They are the front-line people. They get called out to the crime scenes. They help the crime scene investigators decide what to send to the lab and what not to send in. They do the preliminary footwork and talk to the police to gather the information, which they then give to us. They consult with us about which cases need to be autopsied."

The police give the MEs information about the crime scene; for example, the number of shell casings recovered in a shooting. "That's so we will know to be looking at how many times the person was shot and whether it matches the number of

When I was a pathology resident in training,

I had an opportunity to moonlight as a

part-time medical examiner.

Named Assistant Chief
Medical Examiner for
Virginia's Tidewater
District

Has baby girl
Lectures and
teaches

shell casings at the scene. We can tell police things that will help them solve the case, like how far the gun was from the victim when it was fired. We can go to any crime scene we want to, but there isn't enough time to visit every one, so we only go if there is something we need to see to help us understand what might have happened to the person."

Each of the other state district offices has three assistant chief MEs, but Leah's region has only two right now. She and her partner share the workload. "Monday is usually our busiest day. We work six days a week. My partner and I alternate being 'on call' every other weekend and every other night. That means they call us if there is a body that needs to be sent in for autopsy over the weekend. When we are 'on call' we come in on Saturday morning to do autopsies and stay until we are finished. We don't usually work Sundays. If somebody gets shot or killed or drops dead after about 8:00 a.m. Saturday morning, their autopsy usually gets put off until Monday. Plus, there is all of Sunday when people can get shot or stabbed or killed for the Monday autopsies."

It's never the same thing twice.

You get a lot of surprises and you are never bored.

60

Finding the Cause of Death

Autopsies are done first thing in the morning, so Monday mornings can be busy. Leah wears surgical scrub clothes and a surgical barrier gown when she does her autopsies. She has medical students or an assistant helping her. She looks for wounds, bruises, or unusual marks on the body and dissects the organs to find out what they contain—disease, abnormalities, or injuries. Blood and other body fluids are sent to a toxicology laboratory for testing for the presence of drugs and alcohol.

The time it takes to do an autopsy depends on the type of case. With a simple gunshot wound to the head or chest, the autopsy might take an hour. But some cases take much longer. For example, for a person who was beaten and stabbed numerous times, Leah has to document each of the bruises and wounds. This can take hours. She has to measure the injury, photograph it, draw it on a diagram, and interpret it in her own

CAREER CHECKLIST

You'll like this job if you …

- Are curious about all kinds of things

- Can look at the big picture rather than just the details

- Are skeptical, don't believe everything you hear

- Have a strong stomach, won't mind cutting on dead bodies

- Are tenacious, can just keep probing until you find the answers

- Are a good leader who could supervise others effectively

- Are willing to put in the years and hard work it takes to be a doctor

mind. She has to answer the questions: How did this occur? Is this consistent with what the police say happened? Is it consistent with the weapon that the police think was used in the killing? Leah will speak into a microphone connected to a tape recorder to document her findings on tape after she does the autopsy.

Paperwork and Consulting

When the autopsies are completed for the day, Leah tackles the paperwork. That could mean proofreading the transcription of one of the au-

topsy tapes, looking at microscopic slides, reviewing tests for drugs and alcohol done by the toxicology lab, or writing reports.

Occasionally Leah will have to consult with pathologists on staff at the medical school hospital across the street. "When I am autopsying somebody, I might come across something unusual, like a tumor the person didn't know they had and were never treated for. I will take microscopic slides, photos, or x-rays across the street to show to a specialist so I can get the information I need to write my report. I might have to consult with a radiologist, who might look at x-rays of a child who was beaten, or a brain specialist, who could tell me about a tumor in the brain."

Leah also might call a detective on the case to ask a question if she finds something unusual during an autopsy. For example, she might ask the detective what happened to the person's clothes if there are gunshot wounds or stabs to the body and the clothing has not been brought into the laboratory.

Lots of Additional Duties

Both Leah and her partner serve on state fatality teams formed to investigate why certain types of death happen more than they should. Leah serves on the Fetal Infant Maternal Mortality Review Team, which reviews the deaths of babies that are born dead or die shortly after birth. The team looks at what happened to cause the baby's death, including prenatal care, the delivery process, and care at home. The team tries to determine whether the death could have been prevented. This information might later be used by lawmakers to change certain laws or by the state to initiate programs to prevent these deaths. Leah also works with a group that is studying domestic violence—individuals attacked or killed by a girlfriend, brother, husband, wife, or boyfriend.

Leah often teaches classes about forensic pathology for the Police Academy and the Forensic Science Institute. She also speaks at middle

GROUNDBREAKERS
Los Angeles Pathologist

Edith Claypole, born in 1870, specialized in pathology studies at the University of California at Los Angeles after teaching physiology at Wellesley College. From 1902 to 1911 (first on a part-time basis while she completed her degree), Claypole was a pathologist in Pasadena and Los Angeles. In 1912 she joined the Department of Pathology at the University of California as a volunteer. She was a research associate until her death from typhoid fever, contacted while doing work on the typhoid bacillus. Claypole's areas of research were blood and tissue histology and pathology.

Source: *Women in Science: Antiquity Through the Nineteenth Century*, Marilyn Bailey Ogilvie

Industrial Disease Expert

Alice Hamilton, born in 1869, studied bacteriology and pathology in Germany despite her family's objections. She became a professor of pathology at Northwestern University Women's Medical School and worked at the social settlement in Chicago called Hull House. Hamilton became interested in industrial diseases and campaigned for safety laws. By 1916 she had become an authority on lead poisoning. In World War I she accompanied Jane Addams, founder of Hull House, to the International Congress of Women at the Hague.

Source: *A Century of Women: The History of Women in Britain and the United States*, Sheila Rowbotham.

schools, high schools, colleges, and service clubs about her work. Right now she also has another responsibility—she is preparing for a national convention of medical examiners that will be held in Virginia. She is on a committee to help plan the programs and the agenda for the convention.

Only Child and Headstrong

As a girl, Leah, an only child, was always told to study hard. Her father was an elementary school principal and stressed the importance of education. "I was outgoing and friendly, but being an only child I was used to getting my own way and was pretty headstrong. I'm really a social animal, too. I like parties and groups of people."

She went to college at Virginia Polytechnic Institute and State University in Blacksburg, Virginia. She knew she wanted to go to medical school but thought if she changed her mind or didn't get in, she would be a clinical psychologist, and so she had two majors—biology and psychology.

She did get into medical school at the Medical College of Virginia and discovered that she liked cutting and sewing, which surgeons do, and also obstetricians. But Leah knew that she would have trouble getting up at 4:30 or 5:00 a.m. to get to the hospital for surgical rounds, so she ruled out surgery. She also didn't want to be on call all the time to deliver babies, so she ruled out obstetrics. She knew she wanted to marry and have a family, so being a pathologist seemed like a logical choice. She could do lots of cutting and it would allow her to have more regular work hours. Most pathologists' work hours are 8:00 a.m. to 5:00 p.m, with occasional nights and weekends.

When she was doing her pathology residency at the Medical College of Virginia hospital, Leah met and married her husband, who was a computer engineer, but they have since divorced.

"While I was a pathology resident in training the opportunity came up to moonlight—to be a part-time medical examiner. As a medical resident who wasn't making very much

We work every other Saturdays,

but we don't usually work Sundays.

money, the idea of earning $50 per case to go out to crime scenes was appealing, so I was eager to sign on for this extra money. My car was falling apart and this extra money helped me to buy a new one. After three years of doing this work part time, it was time for me to decide if I wanted be a surgical pathologist who would work in a hospital and look at breast and colon cancer tumors or go to crime scenes and hang out with cops and argue with lawyers. For me it was an easy choice. I wanted to be out doing and interacting and not stuck in a hospital somewhere."

Leah got a fellowship to study under Dr. Marcella Fierro, the state's chief medical examiner. "She was my mentor and basically taught me about this field." When she finished her fellowship as a forensic pathologist, Leah got the job in Norfolk as an assistant chief medical examiner.

Leah likes to spend her free time outdoors around her swimming pool with her 10-year old daughter and her dog Lucky. Lucky is a Rottweiler she adopted after people had mistreated it badly. Leah also is a big fan of roller coasters and buys season passes to a nearby amusement park so she can ride frequently. "Maybe it's a stress reliever. But I don't usually get depressed being around death so much. The way I look at it, their suffering is over. Whatever was wrong or horrible in their life is over. The best we can do is be their voice and the last person to speak for them. But every now and then it makes me realize that life is short and there aren't enough hours in the day to get everything done. I see people who never knew it was their last day, and they didn't spend it wisely."

Marjorie Harris

Marjorie Harris

Bloodstain Pattern Analyst, Instructor in Crime Scene Techniques

Senior Forensic Scientist, State of Virginia

Major in Criminal Justice Administration

Bloodstain Pattern
Analyst

Finding Answers in Bloodstains

Marjorie Harris loved reading Sherlock Holmes stories as a girl. She wanted to do what Holmes did—use her powers of deduction to solve crimes. When she was in high school she called the St. Louis police laboratory near her home and asked to take a tour. "I knew I wanted to work in a police laboratory after taking that tour," she says. "I liked the crime fighting aspect of it and I also liked the sciences. I thought, I'll go for the best of both."

Today Margie is a bloodstain pattern analyst and a teacher of crime scene examination techniques for the state of Virginia. One part of her job is to go to scenes where crimes probably have occurred or to look at photographs and materials from those scenes and see what the bloodstain patterns say about the way a crime

Blood Stain Pattern Analyst
Starts at $25,000 to $27,000 per year. Can make up to $80,000 per year with substantial experience.

MARJORIE'S CAREER PATH

Likes Sherlock Holmes as a girl

AA, East Central Junior College, Union, Missouri

BS, Criminal Justice Administration

---

happened. Another part of her job is to teach individuals in law enforcement how to approach a crime scene to look for, document, and collect all types of evidence.

Blood Tells Stories

"Bloodstain pattern analysts look at bloodstains to see the different sizes and shapes and patterns the blood makes. According to those three things we can categorize the stains. From that we can sometimes say what type of event, mechanism, or action happened to the blood to send it into flight. If someone gets shot, it's going to create a totally different breaking up of the blood than someone who cuts themselves shaving and has a large drop fall down from their chin and hit the floor. Someone hit

with a baseball bat will show a different flight path for the blood fluid. We're very conservative in what we say. While we can't look at a bloodstain and say what type of weapon was used, we might be able help investigators limit the scope of what they are looking for. Later, if they do retrieve a suspect weapon we can go out and buy, borrow, or beg a similar weapon and do experiments to re-create bloodstain patterns using this type of instrument.

"Bloodstain pattern analysis is basically a matter of common sense backed by the scientific concepts of fluid dynamics, physics, experimentation, and training. Fluids fly in the air in the shape of a ball. If the fluid hits the surface straight on, perpendicular, at a 90-degree angle, it will just splat. So the stain you have is a

Criminalist,
▼ Independence,
Missouri

Crime Lab Chemist,
▼ Springfield, Missouri

Bloodstain pattern
▼ analysis work-
shop, New York

nice round circle. If the fluid comes in at an angle where the ball makes contact, there will be a smooth semi-circle but then the blood continues to travel because of energy and inertia. I tell my students the difference is like the difference between watching a helicopter land—it hovers and then sits straight down—and an airplane that comes in at an angle and doesn't immediately stop but has to travel down the runway because of energy and inertia. When you see the bloodstain patterns, the 45-degree angle impact starts to look like an egg and the 10-degree angle impact starts to look like a bowling pin. We can actually measure the width and the length of these patterns. The width divided by the length is a trigonometry (math) function that gives us a number. That number is

the sine of the angle of impact. Physics comes into play because if we know the impact angle that this blood struck the surface and if we have enough stains to measure, we can tell where what we call the 'blood source' is in a three-dimensional space. That can be important in reconstructing or re-creating a sequence or series of events or in substantiating or refuting a statement given by the suspect or the victim."

Works Crime Scenes or From Photos

For a long time Margie was the only bloodstain pattern analyst working for the state of Virginia, but she has trained two other people to work with her now. Because the three have to cover the whole state and also do

MARJORIE'S CAREER PATH

Teaches forensic
sciences at
university

Bloodstain pattern
analyst and forensics
teacher

teaching, they must make efficient use of their time. Sometimes they will go to the crime scene and other times they will only get material from the scene. When they don't go to the scene, they use a flashlight and magnifier to examine photographs taken by the investigating officers and/or articles taken from the scene. They might look at clothes from both the

victim and the suspect. "We may be able to tell that somebody is telling the truth, or we may find that the police have to look at that person's statement again.

"What we do is extremely beneficial to the investigation and to the judicial system and the public. But sometimes law enforcement personnel have to release the crime scene before we can get there, like when something happens on a highway or in a business where they can't keep the scene sealed off for a long period of time. Then we have to work with photographs and other materials."

Loves Teaching

Margie teaches bloodstain pattern analysis to both forensic scientists and law enforcement officers. "First we talk about the history of this concept and then we go into the different terminologies used throughout the country. Then we study the different aspects of the analysis. Toward the end of the course I set up a situation scene where there is a re-creation of blood events. The students go in and document it, and then we have a court situation called moot court. I am the defense attorney, which is tough on the students, because I know all the right answers and am probably more skilled than many defense attorneys, who would not know if what you are telling them is on target or not. Even though I've come up against some tough defense attorneys, I think my scrutiny is probably the toughest the students will ever come across. The students have to testify to their finding and to the theory, just as in a real court of law. In forensic sciences, this is required before scientists can actually go into a situation where they would have to work a real case."

CAREER CHECKLIST ✓

You'll like this job if you ...

- Love to solve puzzles

- Are good at math and physics

- Are tenacious and have great patience

- Have a strong stomach

- Can face the worst human beings do to one another

- Won't mind crawling around and getting dirty

- Like to teach

Crime Scene Investigation

Margie also teaches crime scene investigation techniques. She will travel to different parts of the state to give three-day workshops and she teaches at a ten-week course given by the Virginia Forensic Science Academy in Richmond. "We start at ground zero and talk about how you would approach a scene and photograph it; how you would take notes and document a scene; how you would take measurements and sketch the scene; how you would recognize the potential and evidentiary value of evidence at a scene; and what the crime laboratory's capabilities are. For instance, a lot of people don't realize a fingernail can be individualistic evidence. Individualistic evidence is evidence that is unique to the exclusion of all others—the person or the weapon. Class evidence puts it into a group, like 'this particular piece of glass came from a car windshield but we can't say which car.' We can say a fingernail is individualistic because we can say it came from one person and no one else. If you look at your fingernails, you can see little lines in them. These are individualistic to each and every finger, like a fingerprint.

"We talk about how to become familiar with bloodstain patterns, when to call the expert in, when to take impressions of shoes or tool marks, and when to take photos. We'll actually set up a situation and have the students photograph it and critique the photos. We'll do night exercises where the students have to 'paint with light.' We'll teach them how to swab blood samples from different surfaces—coarse wood, metal, bricks, concrete. At the end of their course they have a mock crime scene and they have to do the investigation from start to finish—documentation, notes and sketch, recognize and collect evidence, and fill out a request for laboratory examination, in which they request certain tests on the evidence.

"If we can get the crime scene technician or law enforcement officer who responds to the scene to look at the evidence and say, 'Oh yes, the laboratory is capable of finding out this type of information,' that helps with their decision of what is recognizable as evidence." Margie loves teaching. "When you see their faces light up you know they have really caught the concept and that makes it all worthwhile."

Virginia a Leader in Crime Scene Evidence Courses

Until recently, Virginia was the only state that recognized the importance of a lengthy course in crime scene investigation for law enforcement personnel. "In the last several years other states have called and wanted our curriculum. Virginia has also taken the lead in establishing a DNA databank for convicted felons. If you get a cigarette or a soda pop can or a Tootsie Roll pop from a crime scene, the laboratory can do a DNA profile on it and that profile is put into the databank. It may match DNA in the databank. It's what we call a 'cold hit,' a match when there were no other clues about who the suspect was. That's not confirmation that the person committed the crime, of course, but it is enough for probable cause to seek out this person and find out where they were and get a blood sample to be compared with the DNA from evidence taken from the crime scene."

Sometimes evidence is tainted because it is not handled or preserved properly. Then it is difficult to get a conviction in court. So it is important that both investigators and laboratory scientists know how to treat the evidence properly and to maintain a good "chain of evidence" as it travels through the system.

Starts as Criminalist

After high school, where she was an excellent student, Margie got an AA degree from East Central Junior College in Union, Missouri and then went to Central Missouri State University in Warrensburg, Missouri. She earned a bachelor of science degree in Criminal Justice Administration. She took a lot of physics and chemistry courses in college.

What we do is extremely beneficial to the investigation, the judicial system, and the public.

When she got out of school her first job was with the City of Independence, Missouri Police Laboratory as a criminalist. She collected evidence at crime scenes and also did some analysis back at the lab. "The difference between Missouri and Virginia is the difference between a generalist and a specialist. In Missouri we did have a state police lab, but smaller agencies like the City of Independence Police Department created their own mini-labs where criminalists also analyzed evidence. I did a little bit of everything from A to Z—collect the evidence and then analyze it too."

Margie's second job was in Springfield, Missouri, where she became a crime laboratory chemist. She did tests on all types of evidence and also went to major crime scenes to collect evidence. But one of the downsides of being a generalist in a small Missouri city police lab was that there was a lot of work and not enough people to do it. When the one other person who worked in Margie's laboratory—the serologist—quite to take a job at a chemical company, Margie had to work even more overtime. She got fatigued and stressed. She was teaching forensic science courses at a nearby college, which put additional stress on her. The police laboratory was getting a lot of blood samples from people who had AIDS. Margie realized her work was becoming dangerous because she was tired and stressed all the time and she might make a fatal mistake.

"I thought, 'I need to sit down and write out what my perfect job would be.' I knew I wanted to teach, I wanted to respond to crime scenes, and I really liked doing the bloodstain pattern analysis." Margie had taken some courses in pattern analysis and had always been interested in that aspect of forensics. She even did tests in a little room to see what patterns blood (from animals) would make.

"Within two weeks of making the decision to look for another job, I received a flyer they were sending out to different police departments about a job opening in Virginia. It was a gift from God, actually. When I looked at the job description and at my wish list of the perfect job, they matched exactly. I came to Virginia and applied. They liked the fact that I had a generalist's background and had the bloodstain pattern analysis training. The person I replaced was the only person who did bloodstain pattern analysis for the entire state."

When Margie isn't working, which is infrequently, she likes to watch football and other sports. She also enjoys crossword puzzles and mind teasers. "I really think it keeps my mind sharp and helps me when I try to figure something out at a scene or from a photograph."

The greatest reward of Margie's career is helping to see that justice is done. "I like the challenges of putting the pieces of the puzzle together and following the logical path of deduction to the solution. Also, it's obviously a good feeling when you know in your heart and are convinced in your mind that someone is guilty and what you have done helps to get a conviction. That is satisfying because there is some semblance of justice for the victim and you have stopped the person from doing it again. When I get flustered, like before testimony in court, I think, okay, I'm going to have a mental talk with the victim. If they were alive right now and I was sitting down having coffee with them and I said 'if something were to happen to you, would you want me to pursue this?' I really believe most would say, absolutely, you go for it, girl. So I am doing it for the victims, who can no longer talk for themselves."

Karen Gentry

Karen Gentry

Detective and Forensic Artist, Baltimore County Police

Department, Criminal Investigation Division, Towson, Maryland

Police Detective/
Forensic Artist

She Catches the Bad Guys

Karen Gentry likes the fact that her work as a police investigator gives her so much variety. "I've never had the same type of day twice in all the years I've worked there. It's pretty fascinating."

In her 21 years with the Baltimore County Police Department, Karen has investigated robberies and sex crimes; taught symposiums and workshops for the Baltimore County Police, Maryland State Police, a correctional facility, the FBI, Johns Hopkins University, and many other organizations; worked with prosecutors and judges to change laws on sex crimes; and drawn sketches of criminals who have committed homicides, robberies, rapes, or other sex crimes by interviewing witnesses who saw them. "I don't know too many places where you could

Police Detective/ Forensic Artist
Entry level, mid $30,000 per year range; can make more than $100,000 at the top of a career in local law enforcement.

KAREN'S CAREER PATH

Marries after
high school,
has two kids

Completes police
academy

Works spousal
abuse unit

have such a variety of activities in any one job," she says.

Karen loves the fact that she has to keep learning. She has taken classes or workshops in forensic art and computer graphics, structured interrogation techniques, violent crimes, electronic surveillance, forensic psychiatry, serial sex murderers, family violence, DNA testing, constitutional law, statement analysis, and other

subjects related to her work as an investigator and forensic artist. Right now she is taking courses at the University of Maryland as a part of the Police Academy's program for officers who want to earn a college degree in criminal justice. The Baltimore County Police Department not only reimburses her for the cost of the classes but also gives her time during her working day to attend class.

These days Karen works in the robbery investigation unit. "We handle robberies where the criminal comes into the bank or business threatening or displaying a weapon and demands money. Sometimes victims are shot during the robberies, making them attempted murders, so we handle those too. We also handle kidnappings, home invasion robberies (someone is threatened or assaulted), car-jackings, and street robberies if there is serious injury or a widespread trend.

"We handle the entire investigation—supervising the crime scene, interviewing all victims and witnesses, making the arrests, writing the warrants, packaging seized evidence, interrogating suspects, and submitting evidence for forensic examination. We testify in trials, motions, hearings, preliminary hearings, and before the grand jury.

"We want to keep the crime scene as pristine as possible. As soon as we get there we get as many people out of the area as we can. In a bank, sometimes the robber is given what is called a dye pack with money. Within several seconds of its being given, this pack explodes and sprays red dye everywhere. And it burns. Often as the robber is running, he will drop the money. And

this may expand the parameters that we are trying to protect as the crime scene; for example, he could be out in the street when he drops it.

"The very first thing we do to collect evidence is talk to people who were witnesses to the robbery. The first piece of evidence we have is what witnesses are able to tell us. What have they seen, what have they heard, what was said, where is the physical evidence, what did the robber touch so we can collect fingerprints, where did the crime occur, what was taken?

"Generally we will take notes and also get written statements. But sometimes we can't do that because witnesses are in shock. When we can, we have witnesses write out in their own words what happened so that they can remember it eight months or a year down the road when a person is caught and the trial occurs.

"When the crime lab technician arrives at the scene, he or she collects the fingerprints for us, as well as the evidence and any photos or videos that were taken. We direct the technicians in how to go about this. For example, if the robber picks up a candy bar at a convenience store and lays it on the counter, we'll tell the crime lab technician to collect prints from the counter and also the candy wrapper. We direct the technicians in what to collect because in a business there probably will be all kinds of fingerprints and many of them have nothing to do with the crime. We have to tell the technician in which areas to look, where we think there might be evidence. Each case is different, but most likely the fingerprints will pro-

vide the best evidence. If fingerprints from a robbery are good enough to be retrieved from the scene, they are put into a statewide database of people who have been arrested. The computer will pop out 20 or 30 that are similar, and then our examiners will go through them and do a hand examination. Sometimes we get a positive identification that way.

"Other ways we get leads are from car tags that a witness has seen or from video cameras that businesses have in place for security. Sometimes the business community will offer rewards for information and we'll get a lead that way. We follow up on all the leads from the witnesses and any other leads we get. This will often lead us to the suspect. Then we get a warrant to do a search and seizure or make an arrest.

"Each case is different. Some are very easy to solve and to get the physical evidence and the confessions, and others can take months or even years. There is a basic satisfaction in finding the person responsible and having a complete case that you know is going to result in a conviction. It's nice to be in a position to do something about crime."

Karen has a partner she calls on for help when necessary, but they don't ride together because they each have different geographic areas to cover. Karen is responsible for 270 square miles in rural Baltimore County. Her partner, a man, is responsible for only 30 square miles, but in a more densely populated area. (The ratio of men to women working in the police department is about 10 to 1.)

Karen works either 8:00 a.m. to 5:00 p.m. or 3:00 p.m. to 11:00 p.m. She will work one week on the day shift and the next on the second shift. "We also work a lot of overtime. Sometimes it is surveillance—trying to catch someone. But most of the time it involves the work of having caught the suspect—interrogating them or processing them

CAREER CHECKLIST ✓

You'll like this job if you ...

Want to stop crime

Are even-tempered and analytical

Would be good at interviewing people to get information

Don't mind long hours

Will stay in good physical shape

Could work with mostly men

Will keep learning to keep up with new trends in law enforcement and investigation techniques

Would enjoy teaching

Like to draw

after their arrest or writing up their paperwork. We are on call once every eight weeks, which means we have to work Saturdays those weeks."

13 Years in Sex Crimes

Before she came to the robbery division four years ago, Karen spent 13 years in the sex crimes unit. She worked on cases where adults who were strangers to the victim committed the crime. She would interview witnesses to see what they remembered. "We had what was called an identikit composite. It was a series of facial features drawn on a transparent material that you could lay on top of each other to help the victim describe the suspect. The trouble was that the features were very generic and they were not meant to tell you who the criminal was so much as who he wasn't. In a sex crime the victim has a long time with the suspect, unlike robbery, where it's a matter of seconds. In a sex crime the victim is with the offender for minutes and sometimes longer.

"I saw that my witnesses could do much better than just pointing out generic features. We would start with the identikit, but then they would describe the different features and I would do a freehand sketch based on their description. I would make modifications until they were happy with the likeness. When other detectives saw me doing this, they would ask me to do it for their more serious cases. Then in 1989 I went through the FBI school at Quantico, which has a whole course on forensic art. After the course, my ability to sketch was announced department-wide and they put some rules and regulations around the cases for which I should sketch." These days Karen does one to eight sketches a month for serious crimes. "I primarily do homicides, secondarily rapes and sex crimes, and the third thing is robbery.

Interviews and Then Draws the Suspect

"First I do an interview with the witness. We go through the circumstances under which they saw the criminal, including the lighting and any physical or mental impairments they might have that might limit their ability to view the person, such as poor eyesight or hearing. We also do an alternate order interview where they tell me what happened backwards. This is because of the way things are stored in different parts of the brain. In a backwards interview a lot of things come up. For instance, the witness might remember that the offender had a red hat or was left-handed. Things that they may have thought they already told me but didn't might come out. Sometimes we even do a third part, where the witness puts herself in the perspective of somebody watching. We might get additional things this way, like, 'oh, he had sunglasses on.' Then they are shown the facial features from the kit and we get a general description and I draw the face.

"An interview could take as little as 10 or 15 minutes or as long as an hour and the sketching could take as long as an hour and one-half. It really de-

GROUNDBREAKERS
Mexican Police Commander

Irma Rodriguez, the first female police commander in the Chihuahua, Mexico region and an orthodontist, worked with other investigators to identify rape and murder victims near the Mexican city of Juarez, where many women were raped and murdered in the late 1990s. Rodriguez and her colleagues used computers to reconstruct faces from skulls, compare dental records with bones, and match skull measurements to pictures of missing girls provided by their families. That way, families could at least know what had happened to their daughters.

Source: *Omaha World-Herald*, October 31, 1999.

pends on how many changes the witness wants and how clear the person is about what they want. I won't go beyond an hour and one-half, because beyond that I think they are pretty much grasping at straws. It's a lot easier to recognize a face than it is to recall one, and I don't want them just plugging in a generic feature just to put the feature on the face. It has to look like the person because it will be used as an investigative aid to see if anybody recognizes the person.

"I have had a lot of hits—when somebody calls and says, yes, that's Johnny Jones, and then we show a photograph of Johnny Jones and five other photos to the witness and they identify Johnny Jones."

Karen is the secretary of the International Association of Identification, an organization that has a certification program for forensic artists. To get certified an artist must have had at least five hits, have done it for a minimum of one year, and have a minimum of 120 hours of special training. They also must pass a written examination and take a practical exam,

where a commander pretends to be a witness and gives them features to draw. Some people make a living strictly as forensic artists working with the police but they aren't government employees; they work for themselves and get paid by the sketch.

Marries Early and Tries Different Jobs

Karen grew up in a fairly affluent suburb of north central Baltimore County. She graduated from high school early and got married right away. She and her husband, who was in the Air Force, had two sons. They traveled overseas for his job, and then the family came back to the United States and Karen worked in a number of jobs, including as manager of sales, carpentry and painting, and as a waitress, as she took college classes. A friend suggested she try government work. She applied at the Baltimore County Police Department and liked the idea well enough to go through the testing to get into the Police Academy.

"It was crazy hours in the beginning, and my husband and I had just separated. With two babies at home and being in the academy, it was very demanding, like boot camp and college all rolled into one. You have this very concentrated curriculum that includes some medical training, firearms, emergency driving, training on the laws and codes you need to know for a beat, and how to use computers and to prepare your reports. Today the initial training is 14 weeks long and you earn 43 college credits during that time."

After she completed her initial training, Karen worked a beat in the same precinct that she now covers for robberies. "I worked swing shift and patrol for four years and then took the exam to be a detective. In 1984 I went into a new unit they had started on spousal abuse. We worked on getting judges and prosecutors and public defenders and alternative sentencing programs all on the same page as regards domestic violence. Years ago people would look away, and we were trying to get them to recognize this as a crime problem. I was also on call in the sex crimes unit because they were short-handed. After a year and one-half I moved over to the sex crimes unit permanently."

One of Karen's accomplishments while she worked in sex crimes was to work to get legislators to change the laws so that breaking and entering of a dwelling was considered an aggravating factor for a rape or sex offense. This raised the penalty for the offense to life imprisonment and it raised the status of the arrest to no bail for the commission of this type of crime. When she was in sex crimes, Karen also had responsibility for teaching Baltimore County police officers about spouse abuse. She lectured on spouse abuse to other organizations and police agencies all over the state of Maryland as well.

Karen's kids are grown now. Like their mother, they have an artistic bent. One is a chef and the other designs original furniture. Karen works out at the gym regularly and, although she doesn't have much free time, she likes to scuba dive and snorkel, play golf, and ride a bike. Each year she paints a different bird on her screened porch.

Raemarie Schmidt

Raemarie Schmidt

Supervisory Computer Crime Specialist, National White Collar Crime Center's Computer Crime Section, Fairmont, West Virginia

Major in Chemistry

Computer Forensic Specialist/Instructor

Computer Evidence Expert

Raemarie Schmidt was one of the first people to learn about computer forensics and to set up a computer forensics section at a state crime laboratory. Raemarie's experience and education—a blend of forensic science and computer knowledge—put her at the forefront of the relatively new profession of computer forensics.

A computer forensic specialist works to preserve and recover evidence that resides on a computer and might be used in the prosecution of a crime. Raemarie teaches law enforcement officers how to seize computers without destroying evidence and how to recover evidence from computer systems. She also researches new software to document what works in recovering evidence. Her employer is

Computer Forensic Specialist

This is a new field, so check the latest statistics as you get closer to deciding on a college program. Right now, computer crime specialists in government start in the mid $30,000 range. With experience they can make in the mid $60,000 range. In the corporate world, top security and computer specialists can earn more than $100,000 per year.

RAEMARIE'S CAREER PATH

BS, Chemistry,
University of
Wisconsin

Research chemist,
pharmaceutical
company

Forensic
scientist, drug
analysis section

the National White Collar Crime Center, a private, nonprofit organization funded by an annual grant from the U.S. Department of Justice.

If, in the course of an investigation, law enforcement officers learn that a computer is involved when someone commits a fraud or stores records of a fraud, that computer probably will contain evidence that can be used to prove that fraud occurred and how.

When officers execute a search warrant of the premises of someone suspected of fraud, they need an officer familiar with the proper procedures for how to secure the computer evidence and take it into custody, just as they ought to protect and secure any other evidence at a crime scene. There are special procedures that have to be followed to examine computer records that might be used to assist in the prosecution of a crime. Simply booting up an operating system can make changes to the hard drive, so officers have to know how to preserve the evidence they collect.

"When I started with the Center my primary job was to teach state and local law enforcement personnel how to deal with computer evidence—how to successfully seize it, collect it, make a duplicate image of it, and examine it

Sets up Milwaukee computer forensics section

Coach, certification process, IACIS

Teaches evidence preservation and recovery

in a proper manner so the results could be admitted in a court of law," Raemarie says. "Now I still do teaching, but I also do development of advanced training courses. For example, I researched Windows 2000 and Windows NT software to determine the best methods for processing evidence from these two operating and file systems.

"My third job is to recruit and interview candidates who want to be computer crime specialists with the National White Collar Crime Center. Once we hire someone, I get them through the training program and monitor their progress to make sure they become successful."

Raemarie also participates in a national group that is working to develop standard protocols for law enforcement agencies to follow as they examine computer evidence. The National Cybercrime Training Partnership (NCTP) has been working since 1996 to standardize learning objectives, so that an officer who works with computer evidence has a progression of training courses and exercises to become qualified in the examination of evidence taken from a computer.

Many computer crimes involve fraud over the Internet—promising to deliver a product when money is received and then not sending the product. Another big area for computer crimes is child pornography. A third area is using the computer to keep financial records for illegitimate enterprises. "When we look at how to recover evidence, we teach it in a general fashion. It doesn't matter if it is a spreadsheet or database or a picture file. Computer forensics deals with any crime in which a computer is used."

Researches examination techniques for computer systems

Adjunct professor, Computer Forensics, University of New Haven

Raemarie spends about half her time teaching classes that are held in various locations throughout the country. When she is teaching, she starts her day at 7:30 in the morning and works until 7:30 at night. She instructs law enforcement officers from state and local organizations (and sometimes federal agencies) in the different operating and file systems. She also leads students in hands-on exercises. In the evenings she reviews email messages from the office and responds to any emergencies. Early in the morning (class starts at 8:30) she is available to answer questions from the students. The Center's basic course is called "Basic Data Recovery and Analysis." It is a four and one-half day program that starts on Monday morning and finishes on Friday at noon. It is recommended for anyone who might be dealing with computer evidence. The course can be presented anywhere in the country where the law enforcement agency provides a secure environment for the mobile laboratory and laptop computers that travel with the course. The Center also has an advanced course for investigators who want to specialize in computer evidence, held in Fairmont, West Virginia.

"I really love the teaching," Raemarie says. "I enjoy seeing the light bulb go on in the officers' eyes and seeing them get excited about what we can do to recover the information."

In the future there will be university graduate programs that deal strictly with computer forensics.

The other half of Raemarie's time is spent doing research. She works from her home in Seattle, Washington to research different computer operating and file systems and how to preserve or recover evidence using commercially available software tools. She is connected to her office in West Virginia with an instant messaging system. When she is on the computer, she can communicate immediately via instant messages with her boss and coworkers.

Her research is deep and thorough. "I do a lot of reading. For example, when I was looking at Windows NT (a fairly new operating system), one of the first things I needed to learn about was the new technology of the file system. It's a different way of storing data on the hard drive than in other Windows systems. You have to understand how the file system works in order to recover the information. After I had done my reading and research, I installed the operating system and set up a partition with that file system on it. I got a utility program and started looking at the system on a physical level. Then I

CAREER CHECKLIST ✓

You'll like this job if you ...

Want to help fight white-collar and other types of crime

Love computers, will study computer science

Like to solve puzzles

Would make a good teacher

Can do research/work independently

Want to always be learning something new

Are willing to travel for work

right. At the moment we teach only on Microsoft-based products, but when we set up network courses in the near future we will have to learn to teach some other operating and file systems as well."

Starts Out as Chemist

Raemarie started her career as a chemist for a pharmaceutical company and then moved into forensic chemistry. Her scientific background helps her in the work she does today. "I know that you have to set up a standard test platform and you have to limit the variables. When you are testing something, you change only one variable at a time and then you document exactly what happens. Having that scientific mindset and the training in the scientific method has been invaluable."

Raemarie went to a Catholic high school in Milwaukee, Wisconsin and then on to college. When she graduated from the University of Wisconsin with a degree in chemistry, she looked for a job in her hometown. She was hired to

researched what tools are being used to recover erased NTFS files. I set up a test platform and began deleting some files and seeing how different tools worked to recover them.

"A lot of this work is testing the software to see what it can do and if it can really do what it says it can do. I also have to research the new operating systems as they come out. You can read ten documents about a software tool or an operating system and eight of them will say one thing but two will say something else, so you have to get in there and test to see which ones are

work at a pharmaceutical company. But after a couple of years the company was bought and the Milwaukee offices were closed. She was able to get another job with a new regional crime laboratory being built in Milwaukee. She was hired to work in the drug analysis section, a job she kept for 20 years, from 1975 until 1995.

"They were looking for drug chemists and I was a good fit because I had been doing drug analysis for the pharmaceutical company. At the crime lab I examined unknown materials to determine the presence of any controlled substances—white powder to see if it was cocaine, plant material to determine if it was marijuana, and other types of controlled substances like heroin and LSD. After I had worked there for ten years I got additional responsibilities. I interviewed and hired candidates, wrote performance reviews, and was responsible for the computer systems for some of the machines we used in our analyses. When I started with the lab in 1975 we got a gas chromatograph mass spectrometer. It had what was then quite a sophisticated computer system. As I gained more responsibility and ultimately became section head, I was responsible for the maintenance and repair of all the instruments. As new instruments came in I had to learn their computer systems and I had to train other people in the unit on how to use them."

Sets Up Computer Forensics Section

"In 1991 our division administrator attended a presentation by someone who talked about computer forensics. At that time almost all the computer examiners were police officers because the crime laboratories didn't accept computer evidence; they didn't know what to do with it. So the officers were doing the examinations and they established an organization called the International Association of Computer Investigative Specialists (IACIS). The IRS (Internal Revenue Service) was in the forefront of examination of evidence on computers because people were using computers to keep business records and prepare tax returns. One of the IRS officers developing the computer training for IRS agents helped to establish the IACIS.

"The IACIS gave a presentation my boss attended and he thought computer examination for evidence was a great idea but that it needed to be in the crime laboratory because it is a forensic issue and not an investigative issue. IACIS was giving a two-week training course and the division administrator wanted someone from our laboratory to attend, but we only knew about it three days ahead of time and they only did training once a year. One of the newer people in my section was selected to go. He had a minor in computer science and he was single and could go at a moment's notice. I had gotten married in 1975 and had kids at home, so it was more difficult for me.

"He didn't have a lot of forensic experience, but was knowledgeable about the protocols that had to be followed. When he came back from the training he needed someone to help him set up the computer forensics section in the laboratory. Ultimately, because of my long tenure in the drug analysis section and with the laboratory, I was selected to head the project of establishing a section in the laboratory that would examine computer evidence. At the time Florida had a computer forensic section, but I don't know of any other state level crime laboratories that had one. The next year I went through the IACIS training and met another examiner who was doing the same thing in Iowa. He was a serologist, and like me, he was wearing two hats—working in the serology section and setting up the computer forensics section. We established a regional organization for some follow-up training for computer forensics called the Forensic Association of Computer Technologists, or FACT. It's still a viable organization. I did some advanced training for them last year at their annual meeting."

Moves East, Then West

Raemarie moved to the Maryland area and took a job with the Northern Vir-

ginia Crime Laboratory as a supervisor of the drug analysis section in 1995. "My husband and I had divorced and I decided to leave the area." Even though the Northern Virginia lab had no computer forensics section, she stayed active in computer forensics through IACIS, which had developed a certification program. "I was one of the coaches for people going through the certification process."

The next year Raemarie joined the National White Collar Crime Center's computer crime section, which had been started the year before. The colleague who had worked with her to start the computer forensics section at the Milwaukee lab had taken a job there and recruited Raemarie. She arranged with the Center to be able to telecommute from wherever she was

living, regardless of where that might be. She had gotten married again and knew that her husband, in the computer security field, would need to live wherever his job took him. When her husband got a job in Seattle with Microsoft, she moved with him.

Both she and her husband are on the adjunct faculty at the University of New Haven, which has established a certificate program in computer forensics. "They fly us in to teach the classes." In her spare time, Raemarie likes to bike and hike, and she loves to bake. But, she says, "you really can't get away from computers. They tend to be all-consuming."

Amy Wong

Amy Wong

Director, Northern Laboratory, Virginia Division of Forensic Science, Commonwealth of Virginia

Major in Zoology and Biology, master's in Forensic Science, with specialty in Forensic Serology, George Washington University, Washington, D.C.

Forensic Science Laboratory Director

She Helps the Lab Run Smoothly

When Amy Wong was a girl, her mother worried about her because she thought like a "criminal." "Look how easy it would be to steal from this store, Mom!" Amy would say to her mom when they went shopping. But Amy did not turn into a criminal. Instead she became one of four crime lab directors in the state of Virginia, and the only woman director. As head of the Northern Laboratory, Amy is responsible for the day-to-day operations of the laboratory, which employs about 35 people—forensic examiners, administrative staff, and security personnel.

The laboratory takes cases from Northern Virginia law enforcement agencies, which include state, county, city police departments, sheriff offices,

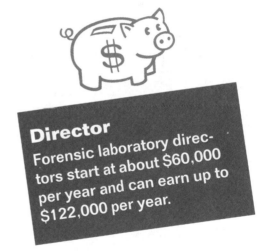

Director
Forensic laboratory directors start at about $60,000 per year and can earn up to $122,000 per year.

AMY'S CAREER PATH

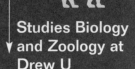

Raised in Queens, NY by Chinese parents

Attends Northfield Mount Hermon prep school

Studies Biology and Zoology at Drew U

fire marshals, medical examiners, and attorney offices for the prosecution and defense. Amy is responsible for all the forensic sections in the laboratory (controlled substances, toxicology, forensic biology, firearms/toolmarks, questioned documents, latent prints). She has to assure that the laboratory does quality work, which includes everything from handling evidence correctly, doing the right tests in the right sequence on the crime scene evidence, working effectively with investigators handling the case, and testifying in a professional and neutral manner in court.

There are eight supervisors in the laboratory, six over the forensic sections plus an office manager and security supervisor. These people report directly to Amy. All members of the staff have to be responsive to law en-

One of the advantages of being a laboratory director is that I am afforded the privilege of impacting policy matters, which often are very important in determining the future direction of the laboratory.

Works at plant store in Northern Virginia, bookkeeping work

Forensic serologist examiner with Ventura County Sheriff's Office

Forensic serologist with Northern Laboratory, VA

forcement agencies that submit evidence to the laboratory. Another of Amy's overall responsibilities is to maintain the accredited status of the laboratory, which means meeting certain standards set by the national accreditation body for crime laboratories, the American Society of Crime Laboratory Directors/Laboratory Accreditation Board (ASCLD/LAB). These accreditation standards relate to the quality of the work generated by the laboratory.

"My work can range from dealing with questions about the kitchen being too dirty, to a defense attorney requesting to see all the case file documents in a case going to trial, to a staff member needing medical attention. I get involved in just about anything that has to do with making the laboratory run smoothly."

The Big Picture

One of the things Amy is particularly focused on is making sure that forensic examiners in the lab approach cases from a teamwork, holistic point of view—that is, from every angle as opposed to one examiner's specialized area of expertise. In the earlier days of forensic science, examiners were often trained in more than one area of expertise and would conduct analytical testing in several forensic areas, from collecting the evidence from the crime scene to doing the blood work, analyzing the fibers, test firing the gun, and doing other tests as necessary. But nowadays examiners are trained to specialize in a particular area because there is so much more to know. Although there unquestionably are many advantages in specialization,

Promoted to
supervisor then
lab director

the danger lies in losing sight of the whole case, of some forensic examinations not being done because no one may think of it. It is important for the specialist to have a basic knowledge of forensic sciences in general and to work effectively as a team member with other examiners, who have different expertise, assigned to a case.

"We want to make sure the examiner is comfortable with the complexities of a case. The examiner has to be able to say to the investigator who submitted the case, 'You submitted this piece of clothing and I see you want me to look at it for blood, but in analyzing it, I noticed this impression on the pant leg which looks like it might be a footwear impression. Are you aware of this, do you want me to have this photographed or sent to another examiner who does impressions

work in order to make sure it is preserved properly before I proceed with my blood analysis?' This is the type of thinking that I expect all of my examiners to have when working a case."

Does Blood Typing First

Amy began her career in forensic science at the Ventura County Sheriff's Office Crime Laboratory in 1981, where she worked in the serology section (which is the genetic analysis of blood, body fluids, and stains on physical evidence related to criminal matters.) She analyzed blood and body fluid and stains on evidence from such cases as homicides, rapes, malicious woundings, and hit-and-runs using genetic marker tests like ABO.

This was before the dawn of DNA testing in forensic cases. If she had stayed in serology, Amy would be doing DNA testing on the evidence today. The approach to cases then and now remains pretty much the same. For example, the evidence still needs to be screened for blood and body fluid stains. Those stains that are most informative to the case are selected; then genetic testing of the selected stains begins. Also, examiners still need to work closely with the investigators on the case, especially if the case is complicated. And like before, a history of the case from the investigator is often necessary for the examiner to best understand what to do with the evidence.

"This is the interesting part of the work. Once you've identified the stains and start running the evidence through the analytical steps, it's not as interesting, in my opinion. That's the mechanical part of it and the part that probably will become automated at some point. The other part, the dealing with the investigators and trying to determine what happened in what

CAREER CHECKLIST ✓

You'll like this job if you ...

Like to solve problems

Can look at the big picture while also paying attention to details

Have good speaking and writing skills

Can work well under pressure and deadlines

Can handle big and little problems resourcefully

Can stand by your own opinion

Enjoy teaching others

Are a little bit of a "ham"

Have a strong stomach for blood and gore

Like science and will go to graduate school

sequence, cannot be automated ever. When the case is complex, what you do is largely dependent on how much case history you have associated with the evidence."

Amy grew up in Queens, New York. Her mother was born in Nanking, China and her father in Hong Kong. The family came to New York because Amy's older sister, who was a music prodigy, won a scholarship to the Julliard School of Music to study piano. "My mother barely knew the English language. She had been born into a fairly well-to-do family in China and when she and my father came here, they really had to struggle in the United States. But even though we didn't have a lot of money, I got a lot of good things as a child. Education was important. I got to take piano lessons and ballet classes. My childhood was pretty packed with school and extracurricular activities."

Prep School Was Hard

For high school Amy went to Northfield Mount Hermon, a private school in Northfield, Massachusetts near where her sister lived after she married. "I did very, very well in grammar school but at Northfield Mount Herman, I barely survived my first year there. I remember calling my sister to tell her I had gotten a C-minus—I had never gotten a C-minus in my life—and she said 'Oh good, you didn't flunk out.' She knew that the kind of scholastic work I was doing in grammar school—although I was getting straight A's—was not really a good foundation because basically we just had to memorize and didn't have to think. At this very good prep school all of a sudden I was asked to read and understand and digest and regurgitate and I wasn't prepared, so I barely made it through that first year. I got better as I stayed there, but I wasn't best in class, which really surprised me because I was so used to being so good at everything."

Amy's parents wanted her to go to an Ivy League college but she ended up instead at Drew University in Madison, New Jersey, where she studied biology and zoology. "I wanted to work as a horticulturalist for the National Botanical Gardens or something like that, but when I got through school there was a freeze on

It wasn't until I was studying for my master's degree at GWU that I became a "good" student. I worked harder in graduate school and did well scholastically because I was really interested in what I was learning.

government hiring." Nevertheless, Amy went to the Washington, D.C. area, where she still thought she might be able to find a government job as a horticulturalist. Instead, she worked in a plant store and got some satisfaction labeling the plants by genus and species. "It was very frustrating when the people who shopped there would take off the labels and everything would get all mixed up."

Discovers Forensics

Then Amy got a job as an accountant and bookkeeper. Her boss liked her and said he would send her for her graduate degree in accounting if she wanted to go to school. "I was walking around George Washington University trying to find the department to get more information and I passed a building called Forensic Science and I thought 'Gee, what's that?' I walked in and met the person who ended up being my research adviser. He suggested I take one class without registering for a degree program and I did and loved it. It seemed to make sense

because my undergraduate degree was all science and yet I wasn't doing science for a living."

George Washington wasn't sure Amy was right for their program at first. She had been out of college for five years and her graduate record exams weren't good. "They said I had to prove that I was sincerely interested. They made me take organic chemistry classes and said, if at the end you are still interested, come and talk to us. I couldn't take the organic chemistry classes and work full time at the same time because the labs were during the day, so I quit my day job and signed up for an eight-week organic chemistry class in the summer. It was a nightmare but I got through it and I got really good grades. Then I took my graduate record exam again and did better. That finally convinced GWU to let me into their forensics program. I value my graduate degree that much more because it was so hard to get into the program.

"When I took my forensic serology class I was really attracted to it. It

There is a tendency to look at cases too narrowly and not appreciate the whole picture. We need to be aware of this and try to see the case from a more holistic attitude.

was like puzzle-solving and I like doing crossword and jigsaw puzzles. I also liked the fact that you could work on a case and then be done with it. I have friends who are science researchers and they never have a definitive answer to things. But in forensics, you work your case, write your report, and go to court and testify and then the case goes away, unless it comes back on appeal."

While Amy was at school she got a job offer from the Ventura County Sheriff's Office in serology and worked with the office for two years. During that time the office sent her to Quantico, Virginia for blood analysis training with the FBI. A person who is now the director of one of the crime laboratories in Virginia recommended Amy for work in the state and when a position opened up at the Northern Virginia Crime Laboratory, she moved back to the east coast.

Amy did blood analysis work in Virginia for nine years and then was promoted to lab director. She doesn't work cases anymore. "One of the advantages of being a lab director is that I am impacting policy matters, which often are very important and determine the future of the laboratory. You don't necessarily do that as an examiner. But working cases has very great rewards as well. You really feel that you have made a difference, especially when you go to testify in a big case."

Getting Started On Your

Own Career Path

Getting Started On

Your Own Career Path

WHAT TO DO NOW

To help you prepare for a career in forensic science or criminal investigation, the women interviewed for this book recommend things you can do now, while still in school.

FIREARMS EXAMINER, LOUISE WALZER

I advise people who have an interest in coming to the crime lab to focus on chemistry and biology courses. If you are more interested in chemistry, then the drug analysis section would fit your needs. If you are interested in DNA analysis, then biochemistry, molecular biology, and genetics are required courses. With firearms analysis, a degree in biology is preferred, although basic chemistry courses also are needed.

Get very familiar with the microscope. Learn how to deal with unknowns (with micro, everything you do is unknown). Start training the mind on observation under the microscope. Study science.

If you're interested in forensics, you may want to try and contact a crime lab for a summer internship. But remember, with chemicals, blood, and firearms in the lab, you have to be aware of the potential dangers and never let your guard down.

The most important thing is to find something you really love doing and to have balance in your life between work and play.

FORENSIC ANTHROPOLOGIST, MARY MANHEIN

Watch *The New Detectives* and similar education programs on TV to get a taste for this type of work. Science courses are extremely important in this field. Try to get some chemistry, biology, and math courses.

Women are beginning to outdistance the men in entering forensic anthropology. It was a male-dominated field for the longest time. The most prominent people in the field today are still the men, but we're gaining.

Some of the jobs are in government agencies, identifying the Korean War soldiers, for example. Jobs in the field of anthropology are often hard to find. However, there are more jobs available in places like Bosnia, where they are trying to identify the war dead. Within universities we've seen a slight reduction in the departments that choose to teach forensic anthropology courses, while at the same time we see an increase in interest not only from the general public but from law enforcement agencies requiring the talents of forensic anthropologists. Some of my students have gone on to set up their own programs in forensic anthropology in a university. That's what I encourage them to do. If you really want to do this, find an area that doesn't have a forensic anthropologist. There are a lot of community colleges in small cities where law enforcement people are crying for people with experience in forensic anthropology. You have to sell yourself. It's not like accounting where there will always be jobs, but you can make your own job for a forensic anthropology career.

INVESTIGATOR—INSURANCE FRAUD, CELESTE DODSON

State Farm offers internships for high school and college students. Investigate these. There are lots of opportunities for investigators in the corporate world, including many jobs in investigating potential insurance and credit card fraud. A number of states require insurance companies to have special investigative units (SIUs); SIUs are a continually growing area. If investigation really interests you, don't let anyone tell you it's not for you. If you want to investigate potential insurance claim fraud, learn the claims process so you know how to read and understand an insurance policy. Each state has rules about the minimum requirements for insuring autos, homes, businesses, etc. Learning your state's requirements is very helpful in understanding insurance investigation.

Read mystery novels. Read the newspaper and try to figure out how things reported there occurred. Talk to police officers that investigate on a daily basis to learn what their jobs are like. The basis of what we do in SIUs is investigation, and investigation always involves the same basic principles—how, when, what, who, where, and why.

People in this profession are always happy to talk to you. Contact an insurance company to get information when you have to write a paper. Also, try games to improve your observation powers. I used to memorize license plates or what people in a room were wearing or how they were acting. Always be curious and have an inquisitive mind.

MEDICAL EXAMINER, LEAH BUSH

Adopt an attitude now that you will work hard in school and later on in life. You will have to work hard at some point in your life if you are going to achieve anything. It's easier to work hard when you are young and have the energy and the spunk. You have to "pay your dues." You can either pay them up front, when you are young, by going to college and studying hard to make a good life and a good career, or you can pay them at the end of your life, when you are an elderly person on a fixed income with not enough money for food and medicine. It's easier to work hard when you are young and able than to be destitute at the end of your life, when you should be living well and enjoying your last few years.

It's not as hard to be a woman in the medical field as it used to be. When I was in medical school there were far more men than there were women, but now there are as many women. You may still run into some stumbling blocks in some areas of medicine—like surgery, for example—because sometimes they still try to discourage women from entering the field. But remember that you can do anything a guy can do. Women are making gains in all areas of medicine. If you want to be a doctor, make sure you have enough math and science in middle and high school, study hard, and don't let anybody tell you that you can't do it because you are a girl.

FORENSIC MICROSCOPIST AND CRIME LAB DIRECTOR, JULIE WILLEY

Watch educational TV shows about forensic science to see if you might like this type of work. Take advantage of every opportunity in school you have to present your ideas to others in formal speeches and presentations. Public speaking is a big part of this job. As an expert witness, you will have to explain scientific concepts to educated people like attorneys and judges and to those who never even graduated from high school.

Stay in your math and science classes. Develop good writing skills. You have to write lots of reports in forensic science.

BLOODSTAIN PATTERN ANALYST AND INSTRUCTOR IN CRIME SCENE TECHNIQUES, MARGIE HARRIS

Get a good foundation in the math and sciences. Also, you will want to establish that you have the stamina for this type of career. If you are the type that gets physically ill when you are asked to cut up a frog in biology class, this career isn't for you. We see a lot of unpleasant things in this work. And even though we wear gloves and protective equipment, we have to climb around and get dirty and get down and wallow in nasty things. Sometimes the smells are pretty strong. You have to have mental stamina as well, because we see the meanness that people do to each other day after day. However, it's a very rewarding career because we help solve crimes.

POLICE DETECTIVE AND FORENSIC ARTIST, KAREN GENTRY

The most important thing is that you don't do anything that would ruin your chances to be hired with the police. Don't do drugs and don't have any criminal offenses on your record, or you probably won't be able to have a career as a policewoman. You also need to get into good physical shape and maintain your body.

The Baltimore County Police has a cadet program for 18 to 21 year olds. Police departments in other parts of the country have similar programs. In our program you can join the police force for three years when you are 18, make good money, and still go to school at night. We switch you around to the different divisions so you can see what police work is all about. You might be working narcotics, in the evidence room learning how evidence is taken in, or in the crime lab learning the techniques of crime laboratory work. You will learn a lot about how police work is done. When you finish you have a really good chance of getting into the police academy.

COMPUTER FORENSIC SPECIALIST AND INSTRUCTOR, RAEMARIE SCHMIDT

Get as many computer courses as you can in high school. Also take lots of science. For college, it would be helpful to have a computer science degree with an advanced degree or certificate in computer forensics. Right now the University of New Haven [Connecticut] offers a certificate in computer forensics. In the future there probably will be university graduate degree programs that deal strictly with computer forensics.

There are many career opportunities as corporate security officers. These people investigate when breaches are made to the company's computer system, in addition to setting up a secure system. Many top accounting firms hire computer specialists to track down and investigate computer crimes.

Most companies will not hire hackers; they will say, "I don't think we can trust you." When you are testing the limits of what you know about computers, make sure you do it within the bounds of the law. Don't try to breach anyone's system unless you have explicit permission to do so. Otherwise, you probably will be ruining your chances to have a career as a computer crime specialist or security expert.

Many law enforcement agencies don't yet recognize computer forensics as a discipline that someone would go into and stay in for a whole career. However, federal law enforcement people are more likely to specialize in computer forensics. Many state laboratory systems are now considering adding a computer forensics section.

FORENSIC SCIENCE LABORATORY DIRECTOR, AMY WONG

Nowadays you have to have a strong science background to get a job as a forensic scientist in a typical crime laboratory. That means chemistry, math, statistics, genetics, and biology. As a forensic scientist, you will need to be able to explain and demonstrate what you did with the evidence and your test results in an entertaining and technically accurate way to the jury, judge, and attorneys in court. There are people I have known who are terrific examiners in the laboratory, but are horrible on the stand because they cannot explain what they do in a clear, organized, and credible manner. Unfortunately, it is not only what you say but also how you say it that is important. The best forensic scientists I know are not only very good at what they do when they are in the laboratory but also are very good at translating that to all different types of audiences, and they enjoy teaching people.

If you know that you hate talking in front of a group of people and cannot be opinionated about what you know, you probably won't fare well in the forensics field. Get on debate teams and talk in front of groups of people whenever you can, to practice your oral communications skills. As a forensic examiner, you will have to come across confidently in court. In the training we do here in Virginia, at the end of your forensic training, you go through a mock trial—that is, a simulation of a court trial—with others playing the part of judge, jury, prosecutor, and defense. We make this as hard as we can on you. This is one of the worst experiences we put our examiners through because, if you are going to fall apart on the witness stand, we want you to do it during your training, as opposed to in a real-life court trial. We have had people who go through all the training, but then cannot do well in the mock trial, and just quit. You must be articulate and have good critical thought processes to be good in this field.

LATENT FINGERPRINT EXAMINER, ANNIE CARVER-JONES

In this world of followers, step out and dare to be a leader. Invest in yourself. It will pay you for the rest of your life.

You should have an interest in chemistry, biology, physics, geology, and/or law enforcement if you want to be a forensic scientist. Visit a crime laboratory and speak with forensic scientists about career choices in the forensic disciplines. Watch television programs that discuss real-life forensic science cases. Check with colleges for courses offered in forensic science and complete your internship at a local police department laboratory, state laboratory, or a federal agency for "hands on" experience. Also, subscribe to professional and technical journals pertaining to forensic science.

You should also be aware of safety. In my job, I have to be very careful with evidence submitted to the laboratory. Because of the risk of exposure to human blood and other potentially infectious materials, it is essential that I maintain an acute awareness of hazards present in the work environment, and take the necessary precautions and measures to protect myself and my co-workers.

RECOMMENDED READING

NONFICTION

The Bone Lady: Life as a Forensic Anthropologist, by Mary H. Manhein
   (1999). Louisiana State University, Baton Rouge. (Mary explains how
   she got interested in forensic anthropology and what her work entails.)

Scientific Crime Investigation, by Jenny E. Tesar (1991). New York, F. Watts.

Crime Lab 101, by Robert Gardner (1992). New York, Walker and Co.
   (Experiments you can try.)

Threads of Evidence: Using Forensic Science to Solve Crimes, by Herman Silverstein (1996). New York, Twenty-first Century Books. (A good background on the forensic disciplines.)

Fingerprints and Talking Bones: How Real Life Crimes Are Solved, by Charlotte Foltz Jones (1997). New York, Delacorte Press.

Forensic Science: Evidence, Clues and Investigation, by Andrea Campbell (2000). Philadelphia, Chelsea House Publishers.

FICTION

O is for Outlaw, by Sue Grafton (2001). New York, Ballentine Books. (The latest in the series featuring private detective Kinsey Millhone.)

Body of Evidence, by Patricia Cornwell (1999). New York, Pocket Books. (One of several books featuring Dr. Kay Scarpetta, a chief medical examiner in Virginia who solves mysteries.)

The Face of Deception, by Iris Johansen (1998). New York, Bantam Books. (A number of Iris Johansen books feature Eve Duncan, a forensic anthropologist who bears a resemblance to Mary Manheim.)

Total Recall, by Sara Paretsky (2001). New York, Delacorte Press. (Paretsky's VI Warshawski is a private detective in and around Chicago. In this book she grapples with insurance fraud.)

GENERAL REFERENCES

Encyclopedia of Career and Vocational Guidance (2000). Chicago, J.G. Ferguson.

Career Information Center (7th ed) (1999). Macmillan.

Peterson's Scholarships, Grants and Prizes (1997). Princeton, NJ. Peterson's website: www.petersons.com

The Girls' Guide to Life: How to Take Charge of the Issues that Affect You, by Catherine Dee (1997). Boston, Little, Brown & Co. (Celebrates achievements of girls and women, extensive resources.)

PROFESSIONAL ORGANIZATIONS

The Internet is a good place to find out about careers in forensic sciences and investigation. Many professional association sites have sections especially for students. Others have general information in the form of "frequently asked questions" that will help you understand careers in these fields. Search on the name of the organization to find the organization's website. Many sites also have extensive links to other forensic and investigative sites. Here are a few places to get started:

THE ELLIS KERLEY FORENSIC SCIENCES FOUNDATION
(with information about scholarships for careers in forensic anthropology)
> http://www.elliskerleyforensicsciencesfoundation.org

AMERICAN SOCIETY OF CRIME LABORATORY DIRECTORS
> http://www.ascld.org

AMERICAN SOCIETY OF QUESTIONED DOCUMENT EXAMINERS
> http://www.asqde.org

ASSOCIATION FOR CRIME SCENE RECONSTRUCTION
> http://www.acsr.com

ASSOCIATION OF FIREARM AND TOOLMARK EXAMINERS
> http://www.afte.org

INTERNATIONAL ASSOCIATION OF BLOODSTAIN PATTERN ANALYSTS
> http://www.iabpa.org

NATIONAL WHITE COLLAR CRIME CENTER
> http://www.nw3c.org

THE NATIONAL ASSOCIATION OF MEDICAL EXAMINERS
> http://www.theNAME.org

THE AMERICAN ACADEMY OF FORENSIC SCIENCES
> http://www.aafs.org

NATIONAL FORENSIC SCIENCE TECHNOLOGY CENTER

http://www.nfstc.org

NATIONAL INSURANCE CRIME BUREAU

http://www.nicb.org

INTERNATIONAL ASSOCIATION OF SPECIAL INVESTIGATIVE UNITS

http://www.iasiu.com

COALITION AGAINST INSURANCE FRAUD

http://www.insurancefraud.org

INTERFIRE (for improving fire investigation worldwide)

http://www.interfire.org

INTERNATIONAL ASSOCIATION OF AUTO THEFT INVESTIGATORS

http://www.iaati.org

DEPARTMENT OF FORENSIC SCIENCE, COMMONWEALTH OF VIRGINIA

http://www.dfs.state.va.us

INTERNATIONAL ASSOCIATION OF ARSON INVESTIGATORS

300 S. Broadway, Suite 100

St. Louis, MO 63102-2808

INTERNATIONAL ASSOCIATION OF COMPUTER INVESTIGATIVE SPECIALISTS

P.O. Box 2370

Portland, Oregon 97208

THE INTERNATIONAL ASSOCIATION OF FORENSIC TOXICOLOGISTS

Ilkka A. Ojanpera

Department of Forensic Medicine

PO Box 40

FIN-00014, University of Helsinki

Helsinki, Finland

INTERNATIONAL ASSOCIATION FOR IDENTIFICATION

PO Box 2423

Alameda, CA 94501-2423

AMERICAN ACADEMY OF FORENSIC PSYCHOLOGY

128 North Craig Street

Pittsburgh, PA 15213

COLLEGE OF AMERICAN PATHOLOGISTS

325 Waukegan Road

Northfield, IL 60093

NATIONAL FIRE PROTECTION ASSOCIATION

1 Batterymarch Park

Quincy, MA 02269-9101

SOCIETY OF FORENSIC TOXICOLOGISTS

PO Box 5543

Mesa, Arizona 85211-5543

Many forensic professions require certification. If you are seriously considering a career in forensic science, use the Internet to find and review the certification requirements for the organizations below or other careers in which you are interested in after you've started college, or request certification requirements be sent to you:

American Board of Criminalistics

American Board of Forensic Anthropology

American Board of Forensic Document Examiners

American Board of Forensic Toxicology

How COOL Are You?!

Cool girls like to DO things, not just sit around like couch potatoes. There are many things you can get involved in now to benefit your future. Some cool girls even know what careers they want (or think they want).

Not sure what you want to do? That's fine, too… the Cool Careers series can help you explore lots of careers with a number of great, easy to use tools! Learn where to go and to whom you should talk about different careers, as well as books to read and videos to see. Then, you're on the road to cool girl success!

Written especially for girls, this new series tells what it's like today for women in all types of jobs with special emphasis on nontraditional careers for women. The upbeat and informative pages provide answers to questions you want answered, such as:

✔ What jobs do women find meaningful?
✔ What do women succeed at today?
✔ How did they prepare for these jobs?
✔ How did they find their job?
✔ What are their lives like?
✔ How do I find out more about this type of work?

Each book profiles ten women who love their work. These women had dreams, but didn't always know what they wanted to be when they grew up. Zoologist Claudia Luke knew she wanted to work outdoors and that she was interested in animals, but she didn't even know what a zoologist was, much less what they did and how you got to be one. Elizabeth Gruben was going to be a lawyer until she discovered the world of Silicon Valley computers and started her own multimedia company. Mary Beth Quinn grew up in Stowe, Vermont, where she skied competitively and taught skiing. Now she runs a ski school at a Virginia ski resort. These three women's stories appear with others in a new series of career books for young readers.

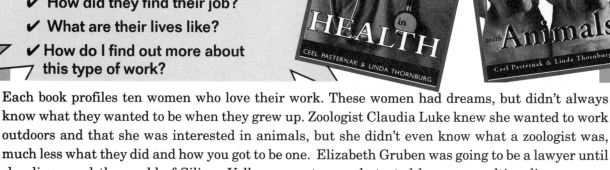

The Cool Careers for Girls series encourages career exploration and broadens girls' career horizons. It shows girls what it takes to succeed, by providing easy-to-read information about careers that young girls may not have considered because they didn't know about them. They learn from women who are in today's workplace—women who know what it takes today to get the job.

ORDER FORM

TITLE	PAPER	CLOTH	QUANTITY
Cool Careers for Girls in Computers	$12.95	$19.95	_____
Cool Careers for Girls in Sports	$12.95	$19.95	_____
Cool Careers for Girls with Animals	$12.95	$19.95	_____
Cool Careers for Girls in Health	$12.95	$19.95	_____
Cool Careers for Girls in Engineering	$12.95	$19.95	_____
Cool Careers for Girls in Food	$12.95	$19.95	_____
Cool Careers for Girls in Construction	$12.95	$19.95	_____
Cool Careers for Girls in Performing Arts	$12.95	$19.95	_____
Cool Careers for Girls in Air and Space	$12.95	$19.95	_____
Cool Careers for Girls in Law	$12.95	$19.95	_____
Cool Careers for Girls as Environmentalists	$12.95	$19.95	_____
Cool Careers for Girls as Crime Solvers	$12.95	$19.95	_____
		SUBTOTAL	_____

VA Residents add 4½% sales tax _____
Shipping/handling $5.00+ _____ $5.00
$1.50 for each additional book order (__ x $1.50) _____

TOTAL ENCLOSED _____

SHIP TO: (street address only for UPS or RPS delivery)
Name: _____
Address: _____

❏ I enclose check/money order for $ _____ made payable to Impact Publications

❏ Charge $ _____ to: ❏ Visa ❏ MasterCard ❏ AmEx ❏ Discover

Card #: _____   Expiration: _____
Signature: _____   Phone number: _____

Phone toll-free at 1-800/361-1055, or fax/mail/email your order to:
IMPACT PUBLICATIONS 9104 Manassas Drive, Suite N, Manassas Park, VA 20111-5211
Fax: 703/335-9486; email: orders@impactpublications.com